WINDOW DISPLAY

DISPLAY
—NEW VISUAL
MERCHANDISING

Tony Morgan

Laurence King Publishing

Published in 2010 by
Laurence King Publishing Ltd
361–373 City Road
London EC1V 1LR
United Kingdom
Tel: +44 20 7841 6900
Fax: +44 20 7841 6910
email: enquiries@laurenceking.com
www.laurenceking.com

Text copyright © 2010 Tony Morgan

A catalogue record for
this book is available
from the British Library

ISBN: 978-1-85669-685-2

Design:
Graphical House
Picture Research:
Annalaura Palma
Senior Editor:
Clare Double
Commissioning Editor:
Helen Rochester

Printed in China

CONTENTS

INTRO—
DUCTION

I can trace my interest in window displays to an early age, when my parents and I would embark on our monthly shopping trip to the closest city (I was bought up in the countryside). Not wanting to get caught up in the throng of Saturday morning shoppers, we would arrive well before the stores opened. My first memory of our retail outings was standing outside British Home Stores (now BHS) waiting for the doors to open to the public. I would gaze into the windows, amazed by the dummies and how lifelike they were. It would be a few years before I discovered that the correct term for them was mannequins.

After leaving school at 16, I went to art college and completed a two-year Diploma in Display and Design – it would be another decade before the term 'visual merchandising' was commonplace in the retail world. After I graduated, I was offered a job at Selfridges in London, which gave me an excellent training. Despite gaining distinctions at college, I still had a lot to learn. For the first six months of my new

career, I cleaned the inside of the windows after the experienced dressers had finished their work. Just being allowed in them seemed a privilege. During my first year I volunteered to work most weekends. I was lucky to have mentors who never tired of my questioning and I learned quickly. I had been adopted by creative geniuses – and hooked by the flamboyant world of window display.

After years of dressing windows and interiors at Selfridges I moved to the fashion office, where I and two others set the trends for the store. Our job involved spending a lot of time at airport lounges. We travelled everywhere to discover things that could be bought, adapted or used as inspiration for Selfridges. During that time I spent weeks in India developing a Bollywood promotion that proved highly successful. 'Tokyo Life', another promotion, saw us touring Japan searching for quirky retailers. A Brazilian-themed event took me back and forth between São Paulo and Rio. While travelling I always made time to visit local retailers and galleries. Apart from the obvious large stores on Fifth Avenue in New York, I found the smaller independent retailers fascinating. From the Geisha Girl store in Kyoto, Japan, which sold only exquisite hair accessories, to being given a viewing of the private collection of jewels and artefacts at the Gem Palace in Jaipur, India, I have been lucky enough to admire incredible works of art in store windows across the world. A trip to New York was always inspiring. Bergdorf Goodman never let me down. One show-stopping window that comes to mind had burnt toast forming a backdrop to the window which, to the customer across the street, appeared as a textured paint finish. I wish I had thought of that one!

Now, as a lecturer and consultant, my love of travel continues. I have consulted in Dubai, Turkey and Sri Lanka, to name a few. I spent a week in Colombo, Sri Lanka, remerchandising an amazing colonial store that sold art and gifts. For my time and effort I received a photograph. Some experiences are worth more than money.

I now prefer to concentrate on teaching and love sharing a studio with eager, creative students who want to challenge the retail world with their inspiring window displays. I never talk to them as an academic but as their visual merchandising manager.

I wrote this book to acknowledge the skills and talents of the hard-working individuals who not only spend hours dressing eye-catching windows but months planning and designing them. To the public, a window display may be just a tool to let them know what is on offer in-store. To these talented retailers, it is never just a job, but a lifestyle.

A store window is no longer just a useful space that a retailer uses to promote their products. As this book demonstrates, the windows of the twenty-first century are dynamic; they are created to enthuse and challenge the consumer and ultimately entice them into the store. Innovation, theatre and knowledge of the market are all aspects that go into conceptualizing these three-dimensional pieces of pavement art. Store windows are now a major marketing tool, used to inspire the masses. The challenge for the visual merchandiser has always been to produce eye-catching window displays that grab the customers' attention and encourage them to shop. Today these glazed canvases promote the store's brand identity, keep the customer informed of fashion trends and ultimately drive sales.

STARTING OUT

The windows featured in this book were designed by the creative retail gurus of the world – artists, most of whom have not been trained in how best to design an award-winning window due to the lack of courses available when they were starting their careers. Their passion has been driven by the product and their enthusiasm for retail, as well as the main component: creativity. These elements sometimes fuse together and innovative individuals are discovered. Often a promising young talent is spotted in the form of a sales associate who is adept not only at selling but caring for their department and initiating creative ideas that impact sales. These gifted young visionaries are often guided to a visual merchandising role. With the guidance of their mentors their creative vision may flourish and they may be given the responsibility of installing a run of windows. Once their talent has been noted they often move on to a competitor and establish themselves. Others may have had a creative foundation prepared for them at art or design college. However, they will undoubtedly still have to prove their worth in the competitive world of retail. Today retail is regarded as a credible career, and visual merchandising courses are springing up across the globe. Visual merchandising can be studied at degree and diploma level, where the experience of the lecturers is passed on to the future creative retail leaders. Many marketing and retail courses also include a small amount of visual merchandising, but this is usually an overview of the subject and will not qualify an individual as a visual merchandiser.

THEMES

Unlike an artist who confines himself to a studio, sketching and contemplating before finally spilling their creative thoughts onto paper over a period of time, a visual merchandiser has to think fast and consider the many obstacles that may hinder the expression of their ideas. To produce a window display that challenges the customer to enter the store, they need to consider many physical and creative elements. An overall innovative idea is a starting point; this will be the theme. This is the creative factor that helps tell the story of what the windows will portray. The theme may support either a visual or written message. This message could be political or social, or simply promote a trend or seasonal event. The theme will undoubtedly include colour, merchandise, props and possibly signage or graphics. Each of these elements will help support the product and thus be the starting point for a window scheme.

SCHEMES

Once the theme has been decided it is developed into a window scheme. The term 'scheme' is used to explain how the window theme may then be carried across more than one window – a run of 20 windows containing the same items will not engage the customers! Assuming that money is no object (a wish for any visual merchandiser), the main component of a great window scheme is the story – the theme it will portray. Creative discipline is then applied; it is never a case of adding and adding until the window is full. An effective display is installed with great attention to visual balance, the use of focal points that aim to draw the customer's eye into the centre of the scheme and then lead the viewer through the contents of the window, and the use of appropriate props that support the product and build up the window scheme. Once these major elements have been established, the dressing of the window can begin. Traditionally the creative force behind a window display was the window dresser, but the term is now redundant. Window stylists, creative direction teams and visual merchandisers now place the products aesthetically so that they appeal to the customers.

The products displayed in a window usually have something in common with the window scheme, be it subtle or abstract. However, as this book will demonstrate, not all window displays tell a story that reflects our everyday, predictable lives. The window display leaders such as Selfridges in London, Printemps in Paris and Barneys in New York use their windows to innovate and inspire. They challenge customers to analyse the store's creativity, not only in terms of their window displays, but also what may be found inside. This retail snobbery may be a way of weeding out who should shop with them, or may simply serve to show how innovative they are as a brand.

Window Display: New Visual Merchandising showcases the best window displays from the world's most successful retailers and talented visual merchandisers. The book is divided into chapters that demonstrate influential tools that you can use to create astounding window displays. It explores how Colour can be used to create atmosphere or provoke an emotion. The Graphics and Photography section highlights how to use text and images to help inform and send a positive message to the customer. Lighting and Technology is about the use of effective lighting schemes and modern technology to create visual impact. The Theatre section proves how an effective and well-considered window scheme can amaze shoppers. The Seasonal chapter shows windows designed to celebrate social, religious or historic events. The Quirky section challenges conventions, with examples of eccentric concepts behind window displays. A final chapter on Trends explores the way a visual merchandiser uses windows to inspire and inform the buyer of the latest catwalk creations.

This book aims to give you an understanding of the elements that are commonly used to create astounding window displays, and show how effective visual merchandising will inspire, possibly educate and undoubtedly encourage sales.

COLOUR

*THE WHOLE WORLD, AS WE
EXPERIENCE IT VISUALLY, COMES
TO US THROUGH THE MYSTIC
REALM OF COLOUR.*
HANS HOFMANN

The most effective window displays are designed with a strong emphasis on colour. A successful window display includes an imaginative colour scheme that will complement the product, help enforce a brand or simply be used to support a window theme. Either way, the visual merchandiser never underestimates the power of colour to aid their creativity. Topshop, London, produced an impressive window in their flagship store that played with this idea. A row of mannequins was positioned in line and spray-painted in a rainbow of colours to make a human colour wheel, starting with yellow and ending with green. Behind them miniature mannequins were lined up, mimicking their larger siblings.

Everyone has a favourite colour. It may be one that calms, excites or simply one that makes up most of their wardrobe. There is also no doubt that colour is a universal instrument used to show or influence emotions. Be aware that colours can have different associations in different countries. For example, in India wearing white is expected when in mourning, yet black usually the respectful colour elsewhere. Customs such as this enforce the impact of colour.

All over the world, red is linked with vitality, the colour of blood (although, interestingly, 'blue' blood runs through the veins of royalty). It is used internationally in traditional Christmas windows, as well as during the sales, to whip people into a shopping frenzy by literally making them 'see red'. Pale green, a signature colour used in Prada's shops around the globe, is also the colour commonly used in hospitals because of its calming nature. A summer window colour scheme is often blue to remind the customer of the clear sunny skies.

A visual merchandiser will carefully consider how best to use this powerful tool. Painting a window in dark colours will give the impression that the window is smaller than it actually is; bright colours will do the opposite and give the impression of space. Darker colours are often used to create dramatic window themes, while bright colours may be used to promote a trend or as a canvas for a children's window display. Reds and oranges were used in the Harrods, London, 'Senses' window scheme to help promote a feeling of warmth, and the backdrop was painted to give the impression of flames flickering through the window. Zara's summer windows, on the other hand, were designed using white as the main colour scheme to support the theme of staying cool in the heat.

A visual merchandiser should never be discreet when applying colour to a window display – using subtle colours will go unnoticed by the passer-by. A gentle winter white or cream is wasted as a wall colour when a brilliant white will suffice and be more dramatic. A true brilliant white has a hint of blue in it to create an icy, cold hue (wedding cakes are a testimony to this; a drop of blue food colouring is added to the icing). Washed-out hues never appear dynamic; bold colour schemes have more impact.

By introducing a well-researched colour scheme, the impression of a window can change dramatically and efficiently. Painting a window's walls and floor is the most cost-effective and practical way of introducing more colour; covering the shell of the window with fabrics is also useful, but it is a more time-consuming method.

Different shades of one colour, used together, can create a visually striking window. The Plummer-Fernandez installation at Selfridges, London showcased an artwork by the designer with no merchandise displayed. The use of the structure set against a backdrop of the same colour turned the whole window into an art piece. Printemps, Paris, used their windows to promote the season's fashion trends by introducing a window scheme of overloaded cars and bicycles, reminiscent of street scenes in Asia. Each window had a different colour scheme played out in bundles of fabric in various shades of the same colour. The mannequins were a contrast in gold. A window scheme as arresting as this demonstrates not only a great understanding of colour and texture, but also the global inspirations of the designer, fusing couture fashion with ethnic eclecticism.

On the same street in the same city, Galeries Lafayette produced a run of windows also themed on Asia, taking Japan as their inspiration. Their window scheme saw brown mannequins with pink hair posing against a backdrop of neon and iconic cartoon characters. The promotion relied heavily not only on clashing colours but on applying colours in unexpected ways. Using clashing or conflicting colours is an effective way of adding a touch of theatre. However, unless planned carefully, the overall window can look messy with no clear structure. A window that relies on an unconventional colour scheme should never outshine the product. Even a window designed with an urban theme and using graffiti as a concept will need to have a colour scheme that is sympathetic to the merchandise.

Monochromatic schemes have been tried and tested in most noted stores. Sticking to black and white is effective, and easy to design with. Whether using the same tints and shades in the merchandise or by contrasting shocking colours, a black-and-white scheme will always create impact. Jaeger, London, produced a monochromatic window scheme using just a single white naked mannequin decorated in black dots that mirrored the concept. Across her shoulder she wore the brand's must-have bag. This striking window was designed in monochrome so that the product stood out, grabbed the customer's attention, and hopefully led them in-store.

There is no doubt that the use of colour can attract attention and send a positive message to a future customer. Most visual merchandisers take inspiration for the colour scheme from the products they are tasked with displaying. On occasion they will create their own colour combination for promotions such as Christmas that do not rely solely on products. Whether following a fashion trend or being bold enough to make an individual statement that draws the eye, colour is by far the most efficient way to create the backdrop for an effective window display.

THIS SERIES OF SPRING/SUMMER WINDOWS FROM *ZARA* HAS BEEN DESIGNED USING WHITE AS THE MAIN COLOUR SCHEME FOR AN EMPHASIS ON STAYING COOL IN THE SUMMER.

THIS STRIKING WINDOW DISPLAY FROM *PRINTEMPS*, PARIS, WAS DESIGNED USING A COHERENT METALLIC COLOUR SCHEME FOR BACKDROP, MERCHANDISE AND PROPS. EVEN THE MANNEQUINS ARE COMPLEMENTARY IN THIS SOPHISTICATED SCHEME.

THIS WINDOW DISPLAY FROM *SELFRIDGES*, LONDON, EMPLOYS A CAREFUL ARRANGEMENT OF PLAYFUL COLOURS. USING BLACK WITH THE BLUES, YELLOW AND PINK HAS CREATED A MORE MATURE COLOUR PALETTE.

JAEGER, LONDON, HAVE USED A STRIKINGLY SIMPLE MONOCHROMATIC SCHEME IN THESE TWO WINDOW DISPLAYS FEATURING JUST A SINGLE MANNEQUIN. THE USE OF THE BLACK DOTS LEADING BACK INTO THE WINDOW CREATES A FALSE PERSPECTIVE THAT ADDS DEPTH TO THE OVERALL DESIGN.

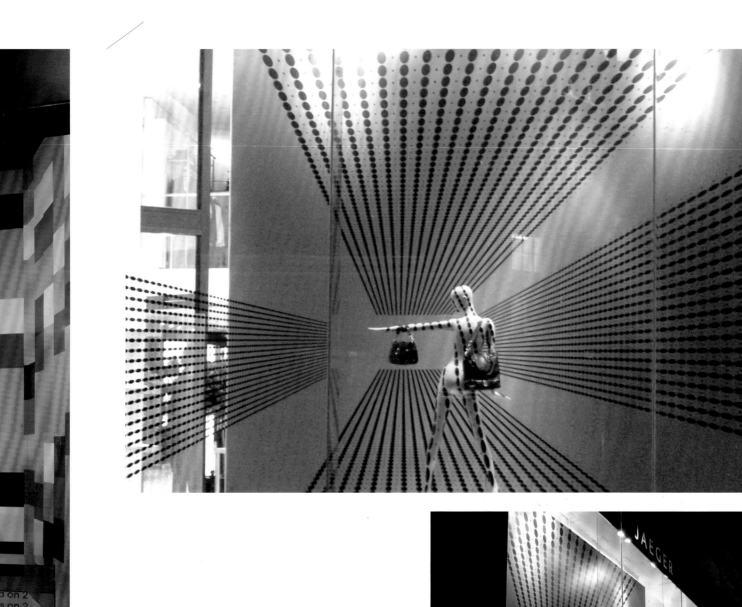

THIS ***SELFRIDGES*** WINDOW IN LONDON WAS DESIGNED USING A COMPLEMENTARY
COLOUR SCHEME – ORANGE AND BLUE (THE MAIN HUE OF THE MANNEQUINS'
MATTHEW WILLIAMSON DRESSES), WHICH ARE OPPOSITE EACH OTHER ON
THE COLOUR WHEEL. COMPLEMENTARY COLOURS MAKE EACH OTHER APPEAR
BRIGHTER AND MORE INTENSE.

THIS WINDOW FROM THE *HARRODS*, LONDON, 'SENSES' PROMOTION
DEMONSTRATES HOW THE USE OF WARM COLOURS LIKE ORANGE AND
RED CAN CREATE THE SENSATION OF HEAT.

A PREDOMINANTLY BLACK DISPLAY FEATURED IN *PRINTEMPS'* WINDOW IN PARIS
IS HIGHLIGHTED WITH THE USE OF MIRROR BALLS AND A MANNEQUIN CAREFULLY
PERCHED IN A SUSPENDED CHAIR AND DRESSED IN SILVER.

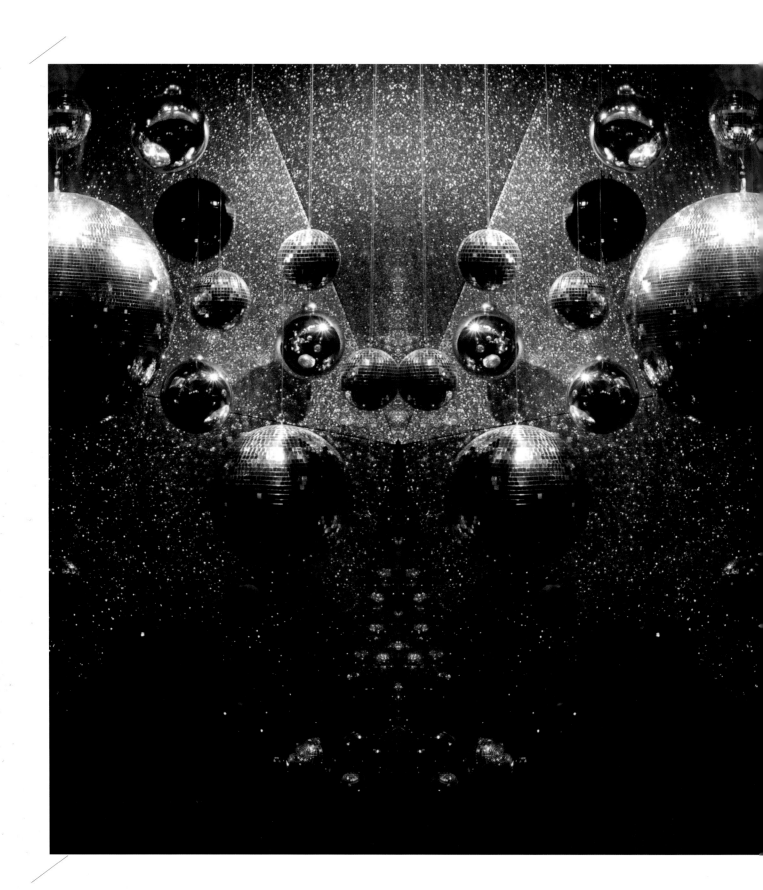

A BLACK-AND-WHITE WINDOW SCHEME FROM *SELFRIDGES*, LONDON, INSPIRED
BY QUEEN VICTORIA. THE MONOCHROMATIC CARICATURES MAKE A BOLD
WALL AND FLOOR COVERING, AND THE BLACK GRIDLINES MEAN THE VIEWER IS
AUTOMATICALLY DRAWN TO THE PIECE OF JEWELLERY DISPLAYED ON THE TABLE.

A SIMPLE WINDOW SCHEME FOR *SELFRIDGES*, LONDON, THAT RELIES ON THE USE OF BLACK AND WHITE TO CREATE DRAMA. EVERYDAY OBJECTS SUCH AS CHAIRS HAVE BEEN USED TO CREATE OPTICAL BALANCE, WHILE THE WHITE GRAPHIC ON THE BACK WALL ADDS DEPTH.

A CLASSIC WINDOW DESIGN FROM *ZARA*, WITH METALLIC SILVERS SET AGAINST A
WHITE BACKGROUND. THE MANNEQUINS, ALSO COLOURED WHITE, BLEND IN WITH
THE BACKGROUND TO LET THE PRODUCT STAND OUT.

THESE TWO WINDOWS FROM *TOPSHOP*, LONDON, DEMONSTRATE HOW EFFECTIVE A SIMPLE COLOUR SCHEME CAN BE. THE USE OF THE RED TEXT ADHERED TO THE GLASS IS PROMINENT AND HELPS PROMOTE THE BRAND, WHILE THE NATURAL WHITES OF THE DISPLAY GIVE A MINIMAL FEEL.

A CONTEMPORARY WINDOW DESIGN BY *PLUMMER-FERNANDEZ* TO PROMOTE *DESIGNERSBLOCK* AT *SELFRIDGES*, LONDON. BY COVERING THE WALLS AND FLOOR IN THE SAME COLOUR AS THE SCULPTURE, THE WHOLE WINDOW, RATHER THAN JUST THE ARTWORK, BECOMES A STUNNING PIECE OF PAVEMENT ART.

THIS WINDOW DISPLAY WAS DESIGNED TO PROMOTE *JOHN LOBB* SHOES, USING THE NEUTRAL TONES OF LEATHER HIDES. THE BLACK CUBES SUPPORT THE PRODUCTS AND DEMONSTRATE THE PRODUCTION PROCESS OF A HANDMADE PAIR OF SHOES.

THESE INSPIRING WINDOWS FROM *PRINTEMPS*, PARIS, WERE DESIGNED WITH THE HUES OF THE COLOUR WHEEL IN MIND. THE SUBTLY DIFFERENT SHADES AND TEXTURES OF FABRIC BEING TRANSPORTED ON VARIOUS VEHICLES CREATE A VISUALLY RICH WINDOW SCHEME THAT IS QUIRKY AND SOPHISTICATED.

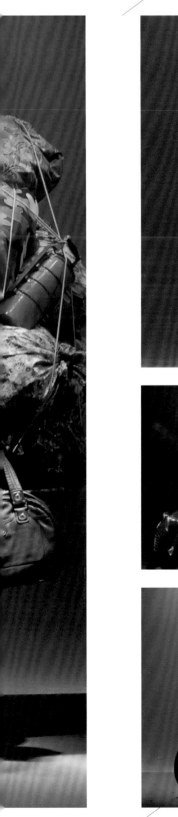

THESE PLAYFUL *TOPSHOP*, LONDON, WINDOWS WERE DESIGNED USING THE
COLOUR WHEEL. THE SCREEN BEHIND THE MANNEQUINS, MADE UP OF MINIATURE
BUST FORMS RUNNING FROM YELLOW TO GREEN IN THE SAME COLOURS AS THE
MANNEQUINS, HELPS SUPPORT THE OVERALL CONCEPT.

A CLEVER USE OF LADDERS IN *TOPSHOP*, WESTFIELD, LONDON. BY SIMPLY PAINTING THE PROPS IN BRIGHT COLOURS AND EXTENDING THEM ALL THE WAY ACROSS TWO FLOORS, THEY ACT AS A SUPPORT FOR THE MANNEQUINS TO POSE ON AS WELL AS HIGHLIGHTING THE IMPRESSIVE SCALE OF THE STORE'S WINDOWS.

THE MANNEQUINS IN THESE *GALERIES LAFAYETTE*, PARIS, WINDOWS BREAK
WITH CONVENTION BY SPORTING PINK WIGS AND WEARING BRIGHTLY
COLOURED CLOTHES THAT DO NOT COMPLEMENT EACH OTHER. THE WINDOWS
DEMONSTRATE AN ECCENTRIC PLAY ON COLOUR.

A WINDOW SCHEME FROM *TOPSHOP*, LONDON, THAT RELIES ON WARM TROPICAL
COLOURS TO PROMOTE THE SUMMER COLLECTIONS. THE COLOURFUL DECALS ON
THE GLASS HELP FRAME THE DISPLAY.

THE COMMON CONNECTION OF COLOUR WITH PAINT IS THE THEME OF THIS *HARVEY NICHOLS*, LONDON, WINDOW. IT TAKES COLOUR LITERALLY IN A STRIKING DISPLAY THAT SHOWS A MAGENTA-SKINNED MANNEQUIN SET AGAINST A PAINT-SPLASHED WALL. THE MANNEQUIN'S WIG REFLECTS THE PAINT DESIGN ON THE WALL BEHIND.

TO CELEBRATE THE CENTENARY OF *SELFRIDGES*, LONDON, THIS SERIES OF WINDOWS PLAYS WITH THE STORE'S SIGNATURE SHADE OF YELLOW IN FUN AND ARRESTING WAYS. MANNEQUINS CLIMB A MOUNTAIN OF BANANAS AND RIDE OVERSIZED RUBBER DUCKS, OR WEAR A BIZARRE COSTUME MADE OF INFLATED RUBBER GLOVES.

Jacket by Dior Homme on 1
Lingerie by Agent Provocateur on 3
Hosiery by Jonathan Aston on 3
Bangle by Fendi on G
Shoes by Christian Louboutin on 2
Gloves by Denis on G

Exclusive Mulberry Bayswater & Coca Cola from
the Yellow Pop Up Shop in the Wonder Room on G

GRAP— HICS+ PHOTO— GRAPHY

*OF ALL OF OUR INVENTIONS
FOR MASS COMMUNICATION,
PICTURES STILL SPEAK
THE MOST UNIVERSALLY
UNDERSTOOD LANGUAGE.*
WALT DISNEY

The last three decades since the arrival of adhesive vinyl, discussed below, have proved to retailers around the world the effectiveness of graphics, signage and photography as part of a window display. There is no doubt that talking to the customer with text is an effective way of communication. Technology has made incorporating graphics in a window display easier, so that it is now a cost-effective as well as efficient tool to deliver a message or to enlighten the customer. The most common use of signage within a window display is to inform the customer of a discounted offer or the price of an item, the location of the product they are viewing or to tell an interesting story about the brand or product. On most occasions it is a winning formula. However, the average customer has little time to study a window let alone read a script, so it is wise to keep the message short and to the point.

Since the invention of adhesive vinyl lettering in the 1980s, retailers have embraced the concept and applied this sticky colourful lettering to their windows. Previously, all signage was either handwritten or produced on a hot letterpress. Once adhesive vinyl was invented, it was not long before photographic images were also reproduced on vinyl. This creation, the decal, is used in most high-street windows around the world. It was used to particular effect by Asprey the jewellers, who applied a decal with a traditional-design etched-glass effect to their London flagship store's Christmas windows (see Seasonal chapter, page 128). The vinyl design wrapped the complete window run and gave the impressions that each pane of glass had been replaced for the Christmas period only.

The most obvious and commonplace use of signage is during the sales. Twice a year, and sometimes mid-season, the windows of all the major high-street stores will surrender to the power of signage. Retailers use this 'window' of opportunity, when their customers have bargains in mind, to help those customers spend their money. Traditionally a store would overload their windows with as many products as they could in the hope that at least one piece of merchandise would appeal to someone. Today, promoting individual items is not as important – retailers rely heavily on announcing that the whole store is on sale. This retail psychology has the customer believing that everything in-store will be reduced (of course, they need to enter the store to find out). Harvey Nichols, London, adopted this method to entice customers across their threshold. They completely blocked out their entire window run with decals that simply stated 'Sale', demonstrating their customary creativity.

Today, many retailers rely on graphics not only to talk to their customers but as an integral part of the window scheme. Many windows incorporate words and photography that are not necessarily there to communicate a message but to form the window scheme itself. Saks Fifth Avenue recently suspended a set of images behind a mannequin, creating a three-dimensional backdrop that not only supported the mannequin but also reinforced the window's theme. They also used text adhered to the glass to send a message to their customers. However, the visual merchandiser generally employs text and images as a secondary visual tool to enhance the window scheme; their main priority is to display the product effectively.

Unlike window signage, photography is a relatively new tool to become commonplace on the high street. Printemps in Paris created a stunning window scheme using large-scale photographs as a backdrop, each of the scenes depicting the interior of a room in a state of chaos. The elegant mannequins placed in front of them created a striking juxtaposition. In New York, Henri Bendel implemented a simple concept to promote their jewellery in an innovative scheme that saw famous Renaissance portraits 'wearing' a collection of the store's earrings. This simple window display would have been very cost-effective, but was also highly creative.

Many of the images that the consumer sees every day (around half a million on average) are part of advertising campaigns. A retail advertising campaign will often be replicated in a window scheme and using the artwork in a window is an opportunity that retailers seldom overlook. Viktor & Rolf used their advertising effectively to promote the launch of their perfume in Selfridges, London, with a decal of the model used in the campaign featured as the main focus for the window display. Any window that relies on advertising as the main content will have to be approved by the brand. Both parties agree on the window design and the length of time it is to be installed for. It is not unusual in large stores for a visual merchandising team from the brand to install and pay for the window. An individual recreating a designer's own branding for a promotion could face legal problems.

Signage and graphics can also be used to provoke a reaction. Louis Vuitton in New York used an urban theme to promote their designer collections, placing graffiti-style decals across the shop front to make it look like the store had been vandalized by a graffiti artist. The graphics were the whole window concept, installed to grab the attention of passers-by.

With today's technology, both photography and text are relatively easy to source, design and apply, whether using large-scale photography as a backdrop or simply on a price label. The invention of the decal provided an invaluable tool for the visual merchandiser. The power of text and imagery is self-evident and will always be considered when a window display is designed. They are an integral part of the high street.

A GOOD EXAMPLE OF HOW TO INCORPORATE GRAPHICS INTO A THREE-DIMENSIONAL WINDOW SCHEME FROM *TOPSHOP*, WESTFIELD, LONDON. WHILE THE LARGE HOOPS ACT AS AN EFFECTIVE PROP TO SUPPORT THE MANNEQUINS, THE ADDITION OF DECORATIVE GRAPHICS ENFORCES THE THEME.

THIS SERIES OF DRAMATIC WINDOWS FROM *PRINTEMPS*, PARIS, USES LARGE
PHOTOGRAPHIC BACKDROPS THAT DOMINATE THE SCHEME. EACH OF THE
PHOTOGRAPHS ILLUSTRATES A HISTORIC-LOOKING INTERIOR, WHICH ADDS
AN ECCENTRIC FEEL.

A STYLISH WAY OF INCORPORATING A DECAL TO THIS *CAMPER* STORE IN LONDON'S WINDOW SCHEME. THE SOFT NEUTRAL TONES OF THE SHOP FIT ARE HIGHLIGHTED BY THE BLACK FAIRYTALE-STYLE GRAPHICS, WHICH FRAME THE WINDOW AND EMPHASIZE THE PRODUCTS.

A COLLECTION OF WELL-POSITIONED BUST FORMS SHOW THE LATEST TRENDS AT *TOPSHOP*, LONDON, IN A DRAMATIC WINDOW SCHEME ARTISTICALLY FRAMED BY DECALS. A GRAPHIC ON THE GLASS MIRRORS THE TWIGS WRAPPED IN LIGHTS IN THE BACKGROUND.

DESIGN DUO *VIKTOR & ROLF* USE STRONG FASHION IMAGES FROM THEIR
ADVERTISING CAMPAIGN AND A FLORAL BACK WALL TO PROMOTE THEIR
PERFUME IN THIS WINDOW AT *SELFRIDGES*, LONDON. THE RIBBON DECAL
IS AN INTERESTING EXAMPLE OF BRANDING.

FRENCH CONNECTION, LONDON, DESIGNED THIS WINDOW USING PHOTOGRAPHY THROUGHOUT THE ENTIRE SCHEME TO CREATE A STRONG FASHION STATEMENT. BY USING THE IMAGES BOTH ON THE BACK WALL AND THE GLASS, THE DISPLAY ENCOURAGES THE VIEWER TO EXPLORE THE DEPTH OF THE WINDOW.

A STRONG MESSAGE FROM *SELFRIDGES*, LONDON. THE USE OF THREE-DIMENSIONAL MIRRORED WORDS STAGGERED TOWARD THE WINDOW GLASS ARE AN IMPOSING STATEMENT. THE MANNEQUIN'S ASSERTIVE POSE COMPLEMENTS THIS MASCULINE WINDOW CONCEPT.

THIS WINDOW PROMOTING THE BRITISH TAILOR *RICHARD JAMES* HAS BEEN INSPIRED BY WORDS IN RED THAT DESCRIBE HIS MISSION STATEMENT: 'I THINK ENGLISH MEN DRESS BETTER THAN ANYONE ELSE IN THE WORLD.' THE SIMPLE DECAL OF JUMBLED WORDS FLOATING ACROSS THE GLASS ACTS AS A QUIRKY TYPOGRAPHIC SCHEME THAT IS OFFSET BY THE ROW OF MANNEQUINS.

WHILE *SELFRIDGES*, LONDON, UNDERWENT SOME REFURBISHMENTS FOR THE
LAUNCH OF THEIR WONDER ROOM, THESE HOARDINGS WERE CREATED TO GIVE
THE IMPRESSION THAT THE COLUMNS SUPPORTING THE BUILDING WERE BUCKLING
UNDER THE WEIGHT, CREATING A SURREAL PIECE OF ART THAT HELPED PROMOTE
THE OPENING OF THE NEW DEPARTMENT.

THE USE OF LAYERS OF IMAGES IN THIS *SELFRIDGES*, LONDON, WINDOW DISPLAY CREATES A THREE-DIMENSIONAL INSTALLATION. BOLD GRAPHICS AND VIBRANT COLOURS GIVE THE ILLUSION OF A LUSH TROPICAL FOREST, WITH VISUAL TWISTS.

A *TOPSHOP*, LONDON, WINDOW INSPIRED BY SAILORS' TATTOOS. TRADITIONALLY TWO-DIMENSIONAL DESIGNS ARE CLEVERLY RECREATED AS THREE-DIMENSIONAL INFLATABLE OBJECTS. THE BIRDS AND THE MESSAGE 'TRUE LOVE' POSITIONED IN THE CENTRE OF THE WINDOW CREATE A STRONG FOCAL POINT.

TOPSHOP, LONDON: A DRAMATIC WINDOW DISPLAY CREATED USING TRADITIONAL WARDROBES PAINTED IN CONTEMPORARY COLOURS. THE PAINT SPLASHES ON THE GLASS AND BIZARRELY PLACED MANNEQUINS GIVE A MODERN ART FEEL TO THE OVERALL DISPLAY.

AS THE NAME OF THE SCHEME 'HALF CUT' SUGGESTS, *HARVEY NICHOLS*, LONDON, CREATED THESE WINDOWS IN TWO HALVES. ON ONE SIDE THE WINDOW DISPLAYS ACTUAL MERCHANDISE, WHILE ON THE OTHER A LARGE GRAPHIC DECAL DECORATES THE GLASS AND COMPLETES THE SHAPE OF THE THREE-DIMENSIONAL PROP.

THIS QUIRKY GRAPHIC ON THE GLASS OF *TOPSHOP*, LONDON'S WINDOW TO
PROMOTE THE DANISH CLOTHING BRAND *PA:NUU* IS A STRONG AND BOLD
ELEMENT OF THEIR DESIGN. USED ON THE WINDOW, IT AIMS TO ENFORCE THE
BRAND AND INFORM CUSTOMERS THAT THE RANGE IS IN-STORE.

ANY STORE THAT SHROUDS THEIR WINDOWS MUST HAVE CONFIDENCE AS A BRAND. A BOLD GRAPHIC STATEMENT FROM *HARVEY NICHOLS*, LONDON, BELOW: A SIMPLE SALE MESSAGE IS ENFORCED WITH OPEN APERTURES FOR THE MANNEQUINS TO STAND IN. BOTTOM: THEY PRODUCE AN EFFECTIVE SCHEME TO PROMOTE A SALE USING LARGE DECALS THAT COVER THE ENTIRE WINDOW RUN.

HARRODS, LONDON, USED GRAPHICS AND SIGNAGE TO INFORM CUSTOMERS ABOUT THEIR 'DESIGN ICONS' PROMOTION. SCAFFOLDING POLES CREATE THE WINDOW SCHEME AND SUPPORT THE PRODUCTS. WINDOW DISPLAYS SUCH AS THESE PLAY ON THE CUSTOMER'S CURIOSITY, SO EXPLAINING THE CONCEPT IS ESSENTIAL.

PRINTEMPS, PARIS, DESIGNED THIS HOMEWARES WINDOW WITH A LARGE IMAGE OF RED TOMATOES TO CREATE A RETRO-STYLE BACKDROP. THE COLOUR IN THE IMAGE HAS BEEN REPLICATED IN THE FURNITURE AND ACCESSORIES.

THE *LOUIS VUITTON* STORE IN NEW YORK APPEARS TO HAVE BEEN SUBJECTED
TO VANDALISM. THE WHOLE FACADE OF THE STORE HAS IN FACT BEEN APPLIED
WITH A VINYL GRAPHIC THAT GIVES THE IMPRESSION OF GRAFFITI – AND
GRABS ATTENTION.

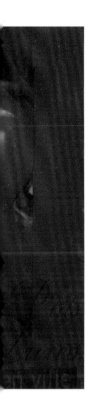

A WINDOW DESIGNED TO PROMOTE LONDON FASHION WEEK IN *TOPSHOP*,
LONDON. THIS DISPLAY HAS BEEN CREATED TO LIST AND ENDORSE THE
COLLABORATIONS WITH THE BRANDS AND THE DESIGNERS THEY STOCK.
AS WELL AS AN EASY-TO-READ LIST ON THE RIGHT, EACH DESIGNER IS
REPRESENTED BY AN ILLUSTRATED MODEL FIGURE WITH MINI PODIUM BELOW.

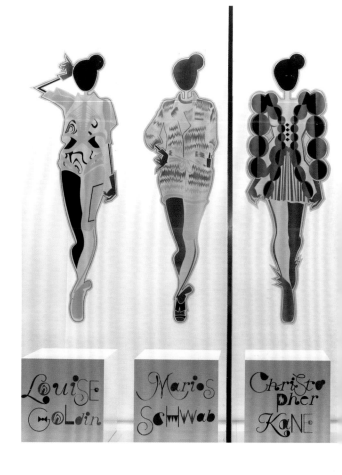

A *FORNARINA* WINDOW FOR *LA RINASCENTE*, MILAN, IN WHICH LARGE PLAYING
CARDS FORM AN IMPRESSIVE BACKDROP. THE TRADITIONAL CARD DESIGNS ARE
REPLACED BY THE BRAND'S ADVERTISING. SMALLER CARDS, STACKED TOGETHER,
MAKE TABLES TO HOLD ACCESSORIES.

THE *RALPH LAUREN* STORE IN LONDON USES GRAPHICS IN A BOLD WAY TO
PROMOTE THEIR ASSOCIATION WITH THE WIMBLEDON TENNIS CHAMPIONSHIPS.
USING THE IMAGE DOUBLE-HEIGHT AND ACROSS BOTH SIDES OF THE STORE HELPS
PUBLICIZE THE MESSAGE TO ALL CUSTOMERS.

A STRIKING WINDOW DISPLAY FROM *SAKS FIFTH AVENUE*, NEW YORK. SECTIONS OF A SIMPLE GRAPHIC HAVE BEEN HUNG AT DIFFERENT ANGLES, TOGETHER FORMING ONE STRONG IMAGE. THE TEXT ON THE GLASS HELPS SUPPORT THE SEASON'S TRENDS.

THIS *TOPSHOP*, LONDON, WINDOW, IN WHICH CUSTOMERS WERE GIVEN THE OPPORTUNITY TO TAKE A PICTURE OF THEMSELVES, WAS DESIGNED IN COLLABORATION WITH NOTED PHOTOGRAPHER *HELMUT NEWTON*. THE PROMOTION PROVED A POPULAR FOOTFALL DRIVER FOR THE STORE. THE STRONG PHOTOGRAPHY AND A MESSAGE ON THE GLASS EXPLAINED THE IDEA.

THOMAS PINK, LONDON, TURNED ITS FLAGSHIP STORE INTO A MOGUL PALACE BY APPLYING AN INTRICATE DECAL TO EACH OF THE WINDOWS. THE EFFECT IS EYE-CATCHING. COLOUR-COORDINATING THE MERCHANDISE WITH THE WINDOW SCHEME HELPS IMPLEMENT THE CONCEPT.

A QUIRKY AND EFFECTIVE WINDOW DISPLAY FROM *HENRI BENDEL*, NEW YORK.
THESE PRINTED IMAGES OF RENAISSANCE PAINTINGS COME TO LIFE BECAUSE OF
A SUBTLE DETAIL: EACH PORTRAIT IS MODELLING DIFFERENT EARRINGS FROM THE
STORE'S JEWELLERY DEPARTMENT.

A COMIC-STRIP WINDOW SCHEME FROM *TOPSHOP*, LONDON, THAT CASTS A
SUPERHERO AS A DEFENDER OF FASHION, SET AGAINST A GRAPHIC BACKDROP
THAT EMPHASIZES THE CONCEPT. THE MESSAGES ON THE GLASS ADD HUMOUR TO
THIS QUIRKY DISPLAY.

AN ARTISTIC WINDOW SCHEME FROM *HENRI BENDEL*, NEW YORK, THAT HAS ALL THE ELEMENTS OF A CREATIVE WINDOW: PROPS AND GRAPHICS THAT ENFORCE THE STORE'S STATUS AS A FASHION LEADER.

LIGHT—ING+
TECH—NOLOGY

THERE ARE DARK SHADOWS ON THE EARTH, BUT ITS LIGHTS ARE STRONGER IN THE CONTRAST.
CHARLES DICKENS

Technology plays a major part in all our lives. Most important for the retailer is how it can be implemented to make the customer spend. The item of clothing that shines out at the passer-by from a store window will have been lit with precise expertise – and the technology available does not stop there. Retailers everywhere are always ready to learn what new innovations can bring to their business. Ever since the American entrepreneur Harry Gordon Selfridge introduced gas lamps to his London store in 1909 so that his customers could view the windows even at night, retailers have searched for new technologies to attract shoppers to their windows.

As well as highlighting the products, lighting undoubtedly adds excitement to a window display. Unfortunately, it is also the most overlooked element of a window presentation, often due to financial constraints – an effective lighting rig can be expensive. When used well it can emphasize specific products or flood an entire window so that it stands out amongst the competition on the high street. The Louis Vuitton store in New York took the concept of lighting to the extreme by suspending hundreds of coloured fluorescent tubes in their windows, not just to highlight the product but to attract customers from across the street. Another of their displays incorporated lasers reflecting off strategically positioned mirrors to create a vivid, futuristic window scheme. However, not all window displays designed around a lighting scheme are costly. Simple light bulbs can be used en masse to great effect as Selfridges did, highlighting a dramatic mannequin elegantly poised amongst a shower of light bulbs. Printemps in Paris took the concept one step further by using just the arms of chandeliers, the illuminated crystals hung strategically to create an impressive window scheme.

Using coloured lighting in a window display can add a touch of theatre, but this slightly dated practice has a major failing. While the light may be designed to create a wash of colour over the scheme, it can also alter the colour of the products. A white shirt can easily become a different shade, confusing the customer.

Forward-thinking stores have refined the use of lighting by installing computer software that adjusts the brightness or even the colour of the window lighting depending on the time of day. More light is required during the day, to compete with the sun, and less when it is dark – a concept that needs some consideration and is not always noted. These expensive units can be programmed to ensure that the product and window scheme always stand out.

In 2008, the French designer Dior commissioned Robert Stadler to create and install the windows of the Dior flagship store in Paris. Stadler took his inspiration from the movies, and created a run of windows presenting changing scenes. His innovative designs were created using a one-way mirror film that adhered to the glass. Using a sophisticated lighting programme, he was able to make the products appear and disappear while the customers' own reflections did the same. For the smaller Dior stores around the world, he designed a window scheme that featured a motorized kaleidoscope made entirely of mirrors to continue the theme of different views. His window designs demonstrated twenty-first-century technology fused with creative design.

The visual merchandiser does not only rely on lighting technology to support their windows. The use of movement will always attract the customer's attention, because passers-by are accustomed to viewing static displays. The White Wall Company designed a series of contraptions for Selfridges' 2009 windows, which saw mannequins flying across the display with rotating umbrellas strapped to their backs. A simple turntable such as the ones featured in the Fortnum & Mason windows not only create motion but can also carry a large amount of merchandise that constantly turns, exposing more product than a two-dimensional presentation. The visual merchandiser clearly has to work extra hard to guarantee that the items displayed are focused towards the customers from more than one angle as the stand rotates in and out of view.

Harrods, London, installed a window scheme for their 'Harrods Rocks' promotion that pushed the boundaries of retail technology. They invited their customers not only to view the store's windows but to interact with them by pressing touch-sensitive panels adhered to the window glass to create music. This surely is the ultimate way of getting the customer to engage with the window scheme. As well as proving that they are at the forefront of technological developments, Harrods were able to hold the attention of those customers who would usually stop, admire and walk on. The longer a possible buyer is captivated by a window display, the more likely it is that they will enter the store and spend.

Visual merchandisers are always searching for the latest technology to use as part of their window displays. The use of touch-screen windows is not just a flamboyant prop designed for department stores with large budgets; it is also becoming a regular fixture in estate agents' windows. One can always question 'what next?' with technology progressing daily – but the window displays of the future will certainly be worth looking out for. There are numerous visual merchandising and retail design fairs around the globe, each of which will showcase the latest available technology to help a retailer's window shout out – or possibly even talk to them.

A SIMPLE USE OF STRIP LIGHTING ATTACHED TO A LIGHTING GRID WAS USED IN THIS *SELFRIDGES*, LONDON, WINDOW SCHEME; THE ADDITION OF A MANNEQUIN POISED IN THE RAFTERS ADDS A SENSE OF DRAMA.

ROTATING ILLUMINATED MOBILES SPIN AROUND THE HEADS OF TWO
MANNEQUINS IN THIS WINDOW BY *DESIGNERSBLOCK* IN *SELFRIDGES*,
LONDON, WHICH DEMONSTRATES THE FULL USE OF TECHNOLOGY.

PRINTEMPS, PARIS, SIMPLY USE THE ARMS OF CHANDELIERS TO CREATE AN AMAZING ELECTRIC-LIGHT INSTALLATION IN THIS WINDOW DISPLAY. THE FORM OF THE STRUCTURE, HANGING PERFECTLY ABOVE THE MANNEQUINS, CREATES A STRIKING VISUAL BALANCE.

THE WHITE WALL COMPANY DESIGNED THESE CONTRAPTIONS FOR *SELFRIDGES*, LONDON. THE WINDOW SCHEME FEATURES MANNEQUINS USING EXTRAORDINARY, HEATH-ROBINSON-STYLE INVENTIONS TO TRAVEL THROUGH THE WINDOWS. THE USE OF ANIMATION DREW INQUISITIVE CUSTOMERS TO VIEW THE WINDOWS MORE CLOSELY.

A SINGLE MANNEQUIN IS FRAMED BY A SHOWER OF LIGHT BULBS IN THIS
SELFRIDGES, LONDON, WINDOW DISPLAY. THE DRAMATIC POSE OF THE
MANNEQUIN AND THE RED CURTAIN ADD TO THE SENSE OF PERFORMANCE.

NEON HAS BEEN USED TO OUTLINE THE IMAGE OF ONE HALF OF DESIGN DUO *BRACHER EMDEN* IN THIS *SELFRIDGES*, LONDON, WINDOW DISPLAY. THE STRONG GRAPHIC AND EMPLOYMENT OF ILLUMINATED SIGNAGE HELP THIS WINDOW CONCEPT AND DESIGNER TO STAND OUT.

THESE WINDOW DISPLAYS DESIGNED BY *BETH DERBYSHIRE* FOR *HERMÈS* INCLUDE
HANGING CYLINDERS THAT NOT ONLY LIGHT UP BUT ROTATE. THE MESSAGE CUT
INTO THE CYLINDERS CAN BE READ CLEARLY EVEN WHILE THEY ARE SPINNING.

THESE INNOVATIVE WINDOW DISPLAYS FROM *PRINTEMPS*, PARIS, ARE DESIGNED
USING SIMPLE STRUCTURED NEON SHAPES, FORMED TO INTERACT WITH THE
ELEGANTLY POISED MANNEQUINS. A MIXTURE OF HARD EDGES AND CURVES KEEPS
THE COMPLETE SCHEME ATTENTION-GRABBING.

STEUBEN GLASS, ZURICH, USE AN INSPIRING PLINTH WRAPPED IN NEON LIGHTING TO SHOWCASE A PIECE OF THEIR HAND-CRAFTED CRYSTAL. THE SINGLE UNADORNED LIGHT BULB HANGS ABOVE THE PROP TO DRAW THE EYE OF THE CUSTOMER INTO THE WINDOW.

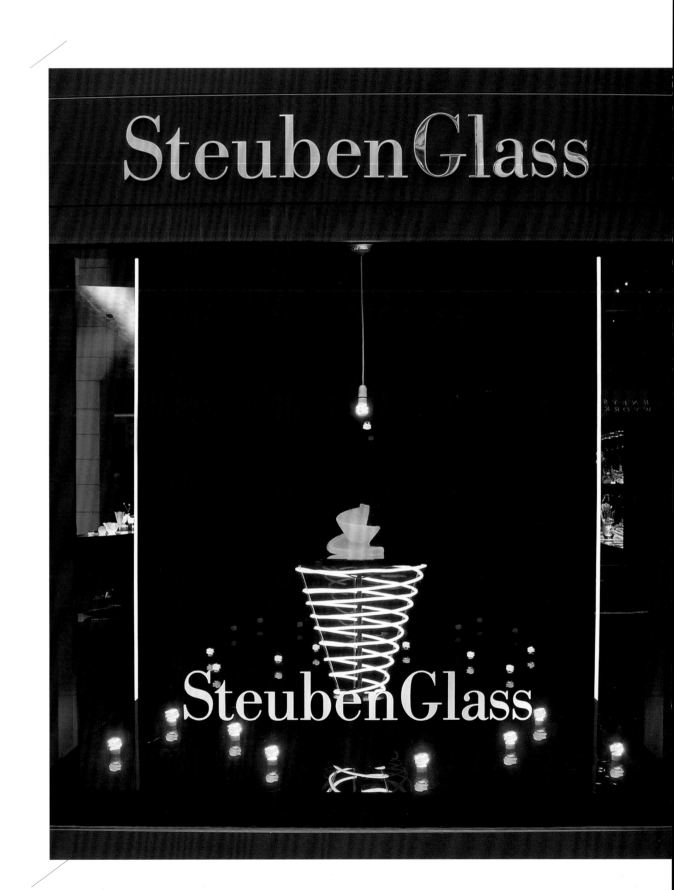

A DRAMATIC LIGHTING EFFECT IN A *HARRODS*, LONDON, WINDOW DISPLAY
HAS JUST ONE MANNEQUIN THAT STANDS PROUDLY AWASH WITH COLOURED
LIGHTING GELS. HER DARK-GREY SKIN COLOUR HAS BEEN CHOSEN SO AS NOT
TO BE AFFECTED BY THE LIGHTING HUES. A PALE SKIN TONE WOULD CHANGE
DRAMATICALLY UNDER COLOURED LIGHT.

TWO SHOWCASES FROM *HARRODS*, LONDON, DEMONSTRATE THAT SMALL
WINDOWS EQUALLY NEED CREATIVE ATTENTION TO MAKE THEM SHINE. A CLEVER
USE OF A LIGHT-BOX ARTWORK SET AGAINST DARK WALLS ACTS AS AN INSPIRING
BACKDROP THAT ALSO EXPLAINS THE OVERALL CONCEPT.

THE *LOUIS VUITTON* STORE IN NEW YORK'S WINDOW SCHEME IS REMINISCENT OF *MISSION IMPOSSIBLE*. ONE LASER HAS BEEN SKILFULLY REFLECTED AROUND THE WINDOW WITH THE USE OF MIRRORS STRATEGICALLY POSITIONED ON THE WALLS. CCTV CAMERAS POINT TOWARDS THE VALUABLE ITEM IN THE SHOWCASE.

THIS *PHILIPS* WINDOW DESIGNED TO PROMOTE THEIR TECHNOLOGY AT *HARRODS*, LONDON, WAS CREATED WITH SIMPLICITY IN MIND. THE BACK WALL HOLDS THE MAIN PROP, A LARGE FLAT-SCREEN TV, YET THE WALLS AND FLOOR HAVE BEEN LEFT CLEAR OF ANY MERCHANDISE.

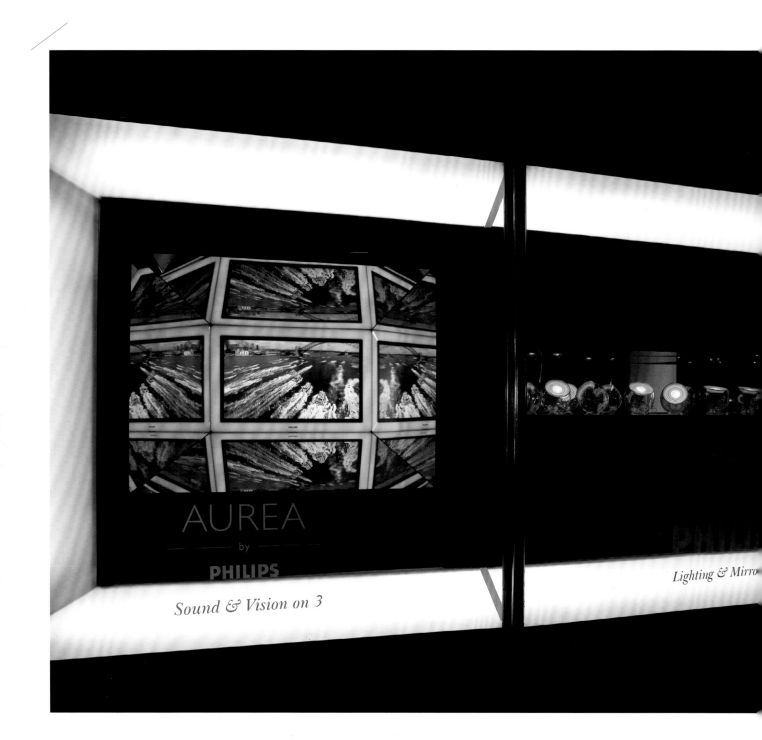

A ROTATING MASS OF *LOUIS VUITTON* BAGS IS THE MAIN FEATURE IN THIS *SELFRIDGES*, LONDON, WINDOW. WHILE THEY ARE STATIC, THE CUSTOMER IS ABLE TO ADMIRE THE BAGS. HOWEVER, WHEN THE TURNTABLE SPINS, THE FOCUS IS NO LONGER ON THE INDIVIDUAL ITEMS BUT ON THE ENTIRE ART PIECE.

THE *DIOR* FLAGSHIP STORE IN PARIS USES COMPLEX TECHNOLOGY TO MAKE MANNEQUINS APPEAR AND DISAPPEAR IN FRONT OF THE PASSER-BY. THE USE OF CREATIVE LIGHTING AND TWO-WAY FILM ADHERED TO THE GLASS MADE THIS INNOVATIVE WINDOW DISPLAY, DESIGNED BY ROBERT STADLER, POSSIBLE.

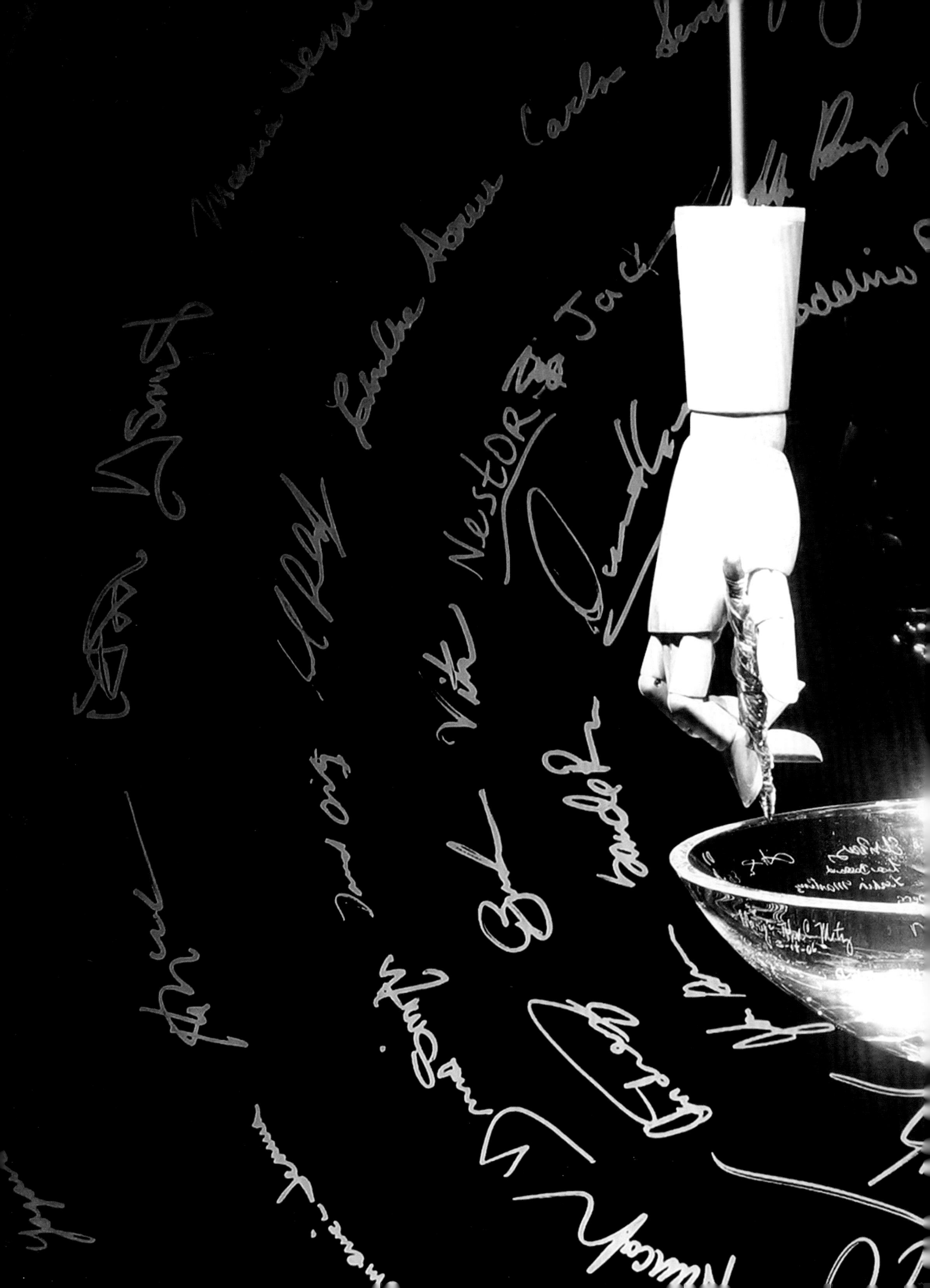

THEATRE

Shoppers living in or travelling to the major fashion capitals of the world will, if they are lucky, be exposed to window displays that surpass any other visual retail experience that they have seen. Discovering a dramatic window display is always a treat. They will witness the product of big budgets that match the skill of the visual merchandiser. When combined, these visual feasts that adorn the facades of the world's premier stores equal the set of any stage show.

Most of these avant-garde pieces of art are confined to department stores, which have large windows for stages and large budgets to accompany them. A production for the likes of Harrods or Bergdorf Goodman, for example, is planned long in advance, and a crew of designers and dressers will be involved. The underlying theme of these sets is drama; the visual merchandiser will have designed these windows with the customers' reaction in mind, hoping that they enter the store and spend. Just as a theatre set will be produced from a concept that may tell a story, so will a theatrical window scheme (whether or not the customers will understand the concept is often overlooked). All of the major components that are required to produce a spectacular window display are utilized, and in most cases exaggerated. Backdrops, either hand-painted or printed, elaborate props, dramatic mannequins and exciting lighting will all be part of the drama.

Often this style of window relies on a strong concept that can be carried across a run of windows. Having more than one window tell a story is a convincing way to ensure that the customer engages with the scheme. With just a single window, it may prove difficult to explain the creative idea behind the design. A window scheme such as Harvey Nichols' 'Depths of the Ocean' in London demonstrates how theatre can be introduced into a window and developed into a complete scheme, here using a run of windows featuring models in designer clothing living in a vibrant underwater world. The clever positioning of the mannequins gives the impression that they are actually submerged in water. The 'Afro Chic' scheme at Selfridges showed a herd of zebra galloping through the windows, with mannequins trying to keep up. The zebra is synonymous with Africa and was a clever call by the designer: it is known across the globe for its origins. It would have been an easy option to use black mannequins, but they were coloured blue, the unpredictable hue adding quirkiness to the overall concept.

It is not unusual to see theatrical window displays designed without the inclusion of any merchandise. These schemes often promote art, which is used as a tool to demonstrate to the public how progressive the store is. The installation 'Chasing Rainbows' by the artist Claire Morgan showcased in Selfridges, London. This intricate piece of art was made from thousands of pieces of plastic ripped from carrier bags and suspended to look like solid structures. Butterflies flew through the plastic, creating an impression of delicate motion. This collaboration with an artist helped enforce how diverse and innovative the store is as a brand.

The fashion emporium Bergdorf Goodman in New York used their renowned creative talents to produce a scheme based on the elements. Each of the windows was designed with fire, earth, water or air as its theme, and the designers pushed their skill and creativity to produce an attention-grabbing run of windows. Each of the windows used fantastically creative props that emphasized the concept and, coupled with an incredible colour scheme and stunning mannequins, these windows must have been an impressive sight for the store's customers when they were unveiled. Ralph Lauren's creative team is another that always impresses with elaborate and detailed windows. They never compromise on props, and many of the items used to support their fashion lines are bespoke, antiques, or perhaps sourced at auction. London's Chapel Street market is a regular haunt for their creative team. Their dedication to making every element of a Ralph Lauren window count is paramount to their success.

Printemps, Paris, created an impressive, dreamlike Christmas window scheme that featured reclining mannequins against forest backdrops. The dramatic element was the mannequins' wigs. These elaborate headpieces were creatively entangled with their surroundings, which included twigs, lights and reindeer antlers. The simple yet highly innovative design made customers stop and admire the beauty of the window dressing.

A dramatic window display is often made up of every creative component that is aimed to shock, or at least cause a reaction. A sure way to accomplish this is to offer something unexpected to the viewer, as Viktor & Rolf did at Selfridges, London. They installed a window scheme that had been designed upside down. The customer saw a complete room set rotated by 180 degrees. Chandelier, furniture and of course the bust carrying the designer outfit were all suspended from the ceiling against a background of upturned windows. A window scheme such as this is not just a tool to impress the designers' following, but to inform them of the creative skills Viktor & Rolf have, whether they are designing an art installation or a couture collection. In turn, such a window sends a message to the store's customers that it supports the very best talent.

A DYNAMIC WINDOW FROM *SELFRIDGES*, LONDON. THE CLASSICAL REARING HORSES AND THE GREEK COLUMN SUPPORTING THE SITTING MANNEQUIN HAVE BEEN BROUGHT INTO THE TWENTY-FIRST CENTURY WITH AN ANACHRONISTIC FLUORESCENT TUBE PLACED IN THE MANNEQUIN'S GRASP.

BERGDORF GOODMAN, NEW YORK, ARE THE MASTERS OF THEATRE. THIS RUN OF WINDOWS DEMONSTRATES THE ATTENTION TO DETAIL THAT GOES INTO THE PLANNING OF THESE VISUAL FEASTS. THE STORE HAS A REPUTATION FOR INSTALLING AMAZING WINDOW SCHEMES, AND THESE COULD RIVAL A STAGE SET. THE FIRST WINDOW SHOWS A DRAMATICALLY POSITIONED MANNEQUIN STANDING UNDER A FOREST WATERFALL. IN THE SECOND WINDOW, A MANNEQUIN

POSES WITH A COLLECTION OF MUTED CONFECTIONERY AND CAKES; HER DRESS LOOKS AS IF IT HAS BEEN CRAFTED FROM ICING. IN THE THIRD WINDOW, A MODEL POSES IN A SUMMERHOUSE FULL OF STUFFED ANIMALS.

A MANNEQUIN LEVITATES IN A DESIGNER DRESS IN THE WINDOWS OF *GALERIES LAFAYETTE*, PARIS. THE MODEL'S WILD HAIR AND ELEGANT POSE CREATE A DYNAMIC WINDOW THAT IS TRULY SHOW-STOPPING.

A DRAMATIC WINDOW SCHEME WITH THE THEME 'ONCE UPON A TIME', FROM *TOPSHOP*, LONDON, TO PROMOTE THEIR CHRISTMAS COLLECTIONS. A GNARLED TREE TRUNK LIKE SOMETHING FROM A FAIRY STORY DOMINATES THE WINDOW, WHILE THE MANNEQUINS POSE ON LOGS OF DIFFERENT HEIGHTS TO MAKE THE MOST OF THE WINDOW SPACE AND HELP CREATE A STRONG FOCAL POINT.

THESE *SELFRIDGES*, LONDON, WINDOWS WERE CREATED USING DRAMATICALLY POSED MANNEQUINS THAT ARE TANGLED IN WEBS OF WHITE VINYL. THE JUXTAPOSITION OF THE STRIKING MANNEQUINS AND ETHEREAL WHITE TRACERY MAKES THE SCHEME DRAMATIC.

AN INNOVATIVE WINDOW SCHEME BY THE DESIGNERS *VIKTOR & ROLF* SHOWING A TRADITIONAL ROOM SET – THIS ONE CREATED UPSIDE DOWN FOR *SELFRIDGES*, LONDON. THIS REVERSAL SERVES TO HIGHLIGHT THE PAIR OF DESIGNER SHOES LYING TEMPTINGLY ON THE 'CEILING'.

A MYRIAD OF COLOURS AND EXOTIC ANIMALS IS THE MAIN CONCEPT BEHIND THIS *BERGDORF GOODMAN* WINDOW IN NEW YORK. THE RECLINING MANNEQUIN ADDS SOPHISTICATION TO THIS ECCENTRIC ENVIRONMENT, WHILE THE PICTURE FRAME ADDS TO THE SENSE THAT THIS IS A DRAMATIC TABLEAU.

THE EFFECT OF MOVEMENT HAS BEEN WONDERFULLY REALIZED IN THIS 'AFRO CHIC' *SELFRIDGES*, LONDON, WINDOW. THE USE OF A BLUE MANNEQUIN RUNNING WITH TWO ZEBRAS ADDS DRAMA, WHILE THE DISORDER OF PROPS AT THEIR FEET SUGGESTS THAT THE CREATURES HAVE JUST BURST ONTO THE SCENE.

'CHASING RAINBOWS', AN INSTALLATION BY *CLAIRE MORGAN* FOR *SELFRIDGES*, LONDON, IS MADE UP OF TORN PIECES OF CARRIER BAG THAT HAVE BEEN STRATEGICALLY HUNG TO CREATE A COMPLEX PIECE OF ART. THE STRUCTURE GIVES THE IMPRESSION OF HAVING BEEN DISTURBED BY THE ARTIFICIAL BUTTERFLIES FLYING THROUGH IT.

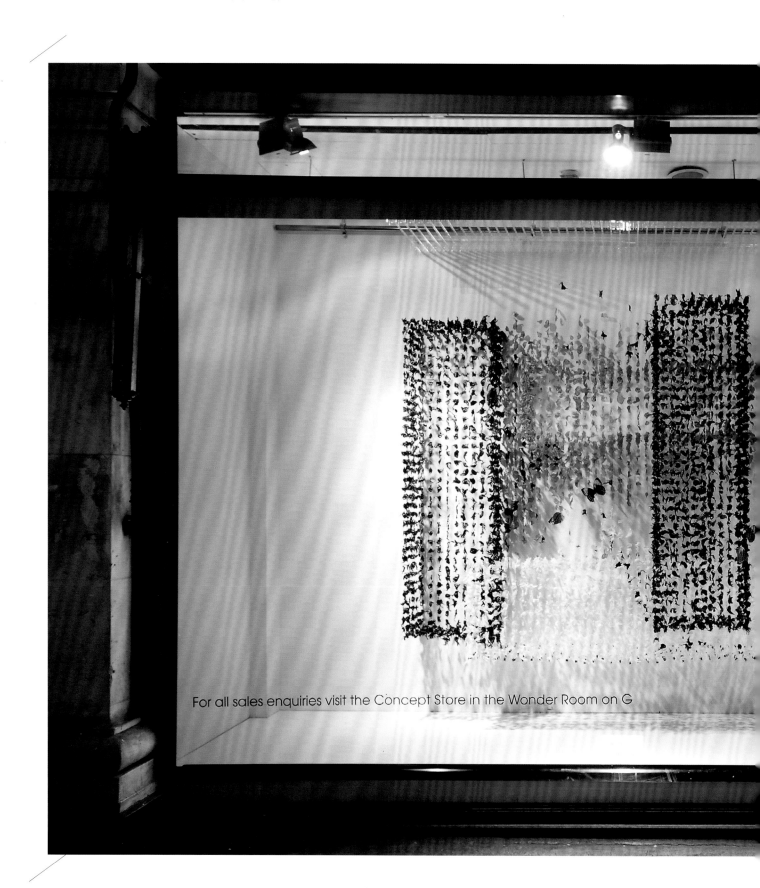

For all sales enquiries visit the Concept Store in the Wonder Room on G

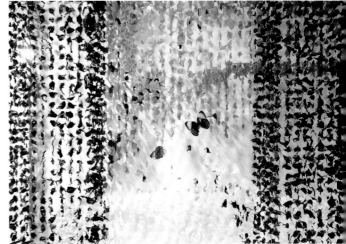

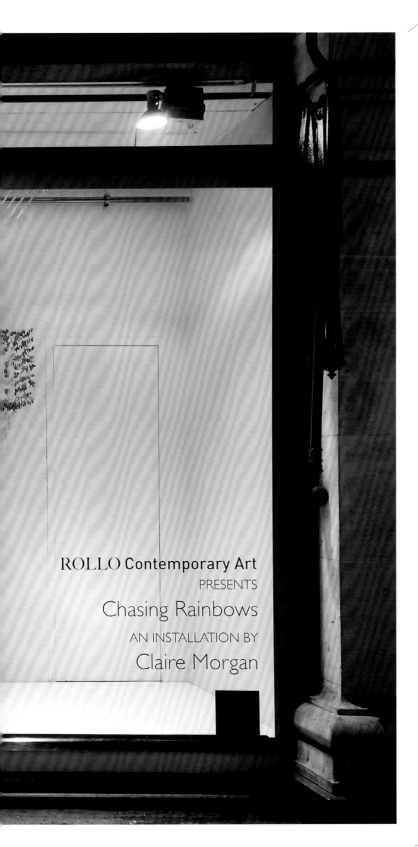

ROLLO Contemporary Art
PRESENTS
Chasing Rainbows
AN INSTALLATION BY
Claire Morgan

AN ECCENTRIC WINDOW CONCEPT FROM THE FAMOUS WEDDING DRESS STORE
KLEINFELD, NEW YORK, SEES MANNEQUINS PLAYING WITH FORGOTTEN TOYS
IN THEIR ATTIC. THE CONTRAST OF SCALE AND THE MANNEQUINS' WISTFUL
EXPRESSIONS MAKES THE VIEWER WONDER.

'DEPTHS OF THE OCEAN', AN UNDERWATER THEME FROM *HARVEY NICHOLS*, LONDON. BOTH THESE WINDOWS USE VIVID COLOURS AND ELABORATE PROPS TO CREATE A DRAMATIC SCHEME INCLUDING FLOATING MANNEQUINS SUSPENDED FROM THE CEILING, GIANT JELLYFISH AND AQUATIC PLANTS CRAFTED FROM COLOURED FOAM.

LITERALLY A COOL SET OF WINDOWS FROM *RALPH LAUREN*, NEW YORK, THAT
SHOWS MANNEQUINS RECLINING ON BLOCKS OF ICE. THE USE OF NEUTRAL WOOLS
AND FUR ADDS WARMTH AND TEXTURE TO A COLD SCHEME.

THE 'ENCHANTED FOREST' WINDOW SCHEME FROM *HARVEY NICHOLS*, LONDON,
SHOWS ELFIN MANNEQUINS SPORTING WINGS AND MAGICAL ANIMALS SET
AGAINST A WINTER BACKDROP. A MANNEQUIN SEATED ON SHARDS OF ICE ADDS
A DRAMATIC ELEMENT.

A MAGNIFICENT RUN OF WINDOWS FROM *PRINTEMPS*, PARIS, DESIGNED TO CELEBRATE THEIR CHRISTMAS PROMOTION. EACH OF THESE DRAMATIC WINDOWS CARRIES THE SAME FANTASTICAL THEME OF MANNEQUINS WHOSE EXTRAORDINARY HAIR HAS BECOME ENTWINED IN THEIR SURROUNDINGS.

STEUBEN GLASS, ZURICH, CREATED THIS WINDOW TO DEMONSTRATE THE ART OF
ENGRAVING. IT IS DRAMATIC IN ITS SIMPLICITY: A SINGLE WOODEN HAND HOLDING
A PEN HANGS OVER AN ENGRAVED CRYSTAL BOWL AS IF ABOUT TO WRITE, SET
AGAINST A BACKDROP OF SIGNATURES.

A SCI-FI FANTASY INSIGHT INTO WHAT THE *SELFRIDGES* CUSTOMER COULD EXPECT IN THE YEAR 2109, 200 YEARS AFTER THE STORE FIRST OPENED. A CONVEYOR BELT SHOWS A SELECTION OF GENETICALLY MODIFIED ANIMALS, WHILE FUTURISTIC SCIENTISTS SUPERVISE, AND A MANNEQUIN RESTS IN HER OWN PERSONAL ENCLOSED GARDEN.

THESE INCREDIBLE WINDOWS FROM *BERGDORF GOODMAN*, NEW YORK, WERE
INSPIRED BY THE ELEMENTS. EARTH, WATER, FIRE AND AIR HAVE EACH BEEN
VISUALIZED WITH THEATRICAL SPLENDOUR. A FLOATING ELEPHANT ENFORCES
THE CONCEPT OF AIR, WHILE OVERSIZED INSECTS SIT WITH COLOURFUL ANIMALS
TO SYMBOLIZE EARTH. AN ELABORATE AMBER FIREPLACE GIVES FIRE, AND
OUTLANDISH CRUSTACEANS DENOTE WATER.

SEASO— NAL

FROM A COMMERCIAL POINT OF VIEW, IF CHRISTMAS DID NOT EXIST IT WOULD BE NECESSARY TO INVENT IT.
KATHARINE WHITEHORN

The changing times of the year are never overlooked by a visual merchandiser. Throughout the year there are many occasions for the customer to celebrate; traditionally, these are days that are supported by religious events such as Easter, the Hindu festival of Diwali or the Islamic celebration of Eid. There are also creative concepts invented by marketeers, who seldom overlook a chance to prey on the public's conscience: Father's Day, Grandparents' Day and Mother's Day. Many of these events are strongly associated with gift giving; a retailer never misses the chance of promoting products that can be purchased as a present for a friend, family member or loved one. It would be naive, however, for a retailer to dedicate an expensive run of windows to an event that only generates sales of greeting cards, which have a small price tag. The majority of stores will dedicate just one window to remind the public of occasions such as Valentine's Day, but plan and install a costly window scheme for a period of weeks that will guarantee sales, such as Christmas. In the United States, Christmas and Hanukkah have fused together in retail environments because the timings coincide, so it is common during the 'holiday' period to see the Jewish menorah candlesticks in window displays.

The most vital season for retailers in Western countries is Christmas, and a visual merchandiser often plans Christmas windows a year in advance.

They will have little time off over Christmas, and will usually work on 26 December dressing the sale windows. Commercial visual merchandisers do not just plan the installation of a window display, but have to consider the removal of their works of art. From late October until the end of December, the windows of most stores on every high street are adorned with decorations and lights, helping to create a positive image of the festive season.

To cynics, Christmas is just a commercial exercise whose only aim is to make money. Others view it as a way to celebrate the season of goodwill. Galeries Lafayette, Paris, use this festive time of the year to showcase their windows. From November to December they have a constant stream of curious customers lining up, cameras in hand, on an annual pilgrimage. However, these seasonal creations are not just a three-dimensional greeting to the public; they are also a commercial method of enticing customers to cross the threshold of the store.

Traditionally, department stores used their Christmas windows to promote family values and, more importantly, to excite children with a large wish list. Toys and gifts usually featured. Many window themes and schemes were created from fairytales and traditional stories – always with a happy ending! Until the 1980s, most of the larger stores stuck to this tried-and-tested method. Fortnum & Mason, London, still relies heavily on their heritage and reputation to present their traditional brand ethos. Their well-planned, ornate Christmas window schemes in their Piccadilly store still stop customers, young and old, in their tracks. Their 2008 Christmas windows epitomized the season, decked in snow and ice, as well as promoting the products available in-store.

Today, possibly because of social change, it is not uncommon to see stores adopting more current themes. Barneys' recent Christmas windows played on the customer's conscience by sending an ecological message, delivered, of course, tongue in cheek. Not only were the windows green in colour; some were even constructed using recycled green plastic bottles. Interestingly, none of the windows promoted any products, which is testimony both to the designer Simon Doonan's confidence and to the trend for prestigious stores to promote their brand image not through products but by creating impressive installations that become the talk of the town. Selfridges, London, showed Santa pushing his

shopping trolley through the aisles of a supermarket and breakdancing on a floor covered in empty glasses. By breaking with tradition but retaining an element of humour, these windows made a big impression and, importantly, appealed to all ages.

Christmas windows are not always just about enticing children, as the British fashion designer Matthew Williamson proves. His London store saw couture mannequins reclining on push-bikes amid a snowdrift and polar bears. The fashion maestro added a touch of British eccentricity by accessorizing the models with polar-bear heads.

Although Christmas windows are the most important of the year for many stores, other events throughout the year are also important to some retailers. Ralph Lauren, London, will never miss an opportunity to create a window scheme that promotes the Wimbledon tennis championships, with clothing appropriate for the occasion.

Valentine's Day may only be promoted for two weeks compared to the two months dedicated to a Christmas display, so astute retailers make the most of this period by promoting non-traditional Valentine's gifts as well as the time-honoured ones. The public rarely notices the swift transformation between window schemes, but a Valentine's Day window like the ones installed in the windows of the renowned crystal manufacturer Steuben Glass in Zurich will be removed and redressed on 15 February with little impact to the business.

FORTNUM & MASON, LONDON, HAVE ADAPTED THE TRADITIONAL CAROL 'THE TWELVE DAYS OF CHRISTMAS' FOR A SEASONAL WINDOW SCHEME. THIS WINDOW HAS A LARGE OPEN BOOK TO HELP NARRATE THE STORY.

TRADITIONAL SEASONAL WINDOWS AT *FORTNUM & MASON*, LONDON. THIS
INTRICATE AND DETAILED SCHEME HAS BEEN CONCEPTUALIZED WITH THE MAIN
ELEMENT OF AN IDEALIZED CHRISTMAS IN MIND: SNOW. THE MINIATURE FIGURES
ILLUSTRATE A STORY BEING TOLD ACROSS THE WINDOWS.

A DRAMATIC CHRISTMAS WINDOW FROM *FORTNUM & MASON*, LONDON, THAT CONTINUES THE THEME OF SNOW AND ICE AND ALSO ROTATES, TO GIVE THE CUSTOMER A 360-DEGREE VIEW OF THE PRODUCTS.

A SOPHISTICATED CHRISTMAS WINDOW FROM *RALPH LAUREN*, NEW YORK.
STYLISH MODELS POSE IN FRONT OF A BACKDROP OF CUT LOGS AND A FLOOR
OF SNOW, WITH THEIR SKIS LEANING AGAINST THE WALL. THIS CONTEMPORARY
VIEW OF THE SEASON SHOWS THE FOCUS ON WINTER SPORTS RATHER THAN
THE FESTIVITIES.

THIS COLLECTION OF WINDOW DISPLAYS FROM *BARNEYS*, NEW YORK, WAS
DESIGNED TO GIVE NOT ONLY A CHRISTMAS MESSAGE BUT A THOUGHT-PROVOKING
ONE, TOO. THE WITTY SCHEME WAS CREATED USING RECYCLED ITEMS – A SERIOUS
MESSAGE DELIVERED IN A QUIRKY STYLE.

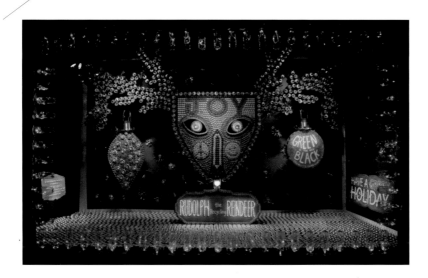

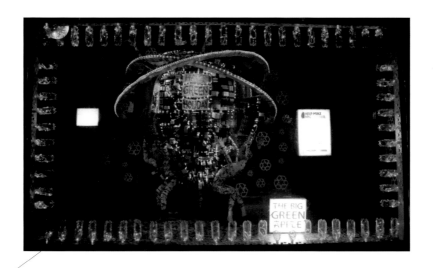

A HILARIOUS MODERN TAKE ON CHRISTMAS AT *SELFRIDGES*, LONDON, SEES SANTA SHOPPING IN A SUPERMARKET. POSITIONING THE FIXTURES AT ANGLES AND THE USE OF OVERSIZED GROCERIES HAS GIVEN DEPTH TO THE WINDOW. THE ANACHRONISM CONTINUES IN THE SECOND PICTURE, WHERE SANTA BREAKDANCES AMONGST A COLLECTION OF EMPTY GLASSES, AGAINST A BACKDROP OF NEON!

A STUNNING FESTIVE WINDOW SCHEME AT *ASPREY*, LONDON. THE ETCHED-GLASS DECAL THAT HAS BEEN APPLIED TO ALL OF THE WINDOW GLASS IS SUBTLE AND ELEGANT, WHILE THE TRADITIONAL CHRISTMAS GARLANDS HELP OUTLINE THE WINDOWS.

ANOTHER MAGICAL CHRISTMAS WINDOW SCHEME DESIGNED BY
GALERIES LAFAYETTE, PARIS, WHICH HAS BEEN DESIGNED WITH CHILDREN
IN MIND. FLOATING BABIES AND FEASTING DOGS ALL ADD TO THE VISUAL
MERRIMENT OF THESE FAMOUS WINDOWS, WHICH HAVE BECOME AN EVENT
IN THE PARISIAN CALENDAR.

A MODERN FESTIVE TAKE IN BOTH OF THESE WINDOWS FROM *PRINTEMPS*, PARIS:
A WINTER FOREST THEME THAT HAS SINISTER UNDERTONES, WITH THE ADDITION
OF THE ANIMAL HEADS INSTEAD OF HUMAN.

A RUN OF DRAMATIC WINDOWS FROM *RALPH LAUREN*, NEW YORK, WHICH CREATES THE IMPRESSION OF A CRISP WINTER NIGHT THROUGH THE APPLICATION OF FROST ON THE GLASS. A STRIKING BLACK HORSE ADDS A THEATRICAL TOUCH.

A REINDEER AND HIS GANG OF SNOWMEN BREAK INTO THE *MOSCHINO* STORE, MILAN, IN THIS QUIRKY WINDOW DISPLAY. THE WINDOW HAS BEEN DESIGNED TO CAPTURE THE IMAGINATION OF BOTH ADULTS AND CHILDREN.

A SPECTACULAR CHRISTMAS WINDOW FROM *STEUBEN GLASS*, ZURICH. THE CHRISTMAS TREE HAS BEEN CONSTRUCTED ENTIRELY OF SUSPENDED, HANDMADE CRYSTAL DECORATIONS.

SNOW AND POLAR BEARS ARE THE MAIN INGREDIENT OF THESE SOPHISTICATED *MATTHEW WILLIAMSON* CHRISTMAS WINDOWS, LONDON. NOT CONTENT WITH THE LIFELIKE REPLICAS, MASKS HAVE BEEN ADDED TO THE MANNEQUINS TO ADD AN ELEMENT OF THEATRE.

THE STANDS SUPPORTING THE CRYSTAL ORNAMENTS IN THIS DRAMATIC
VALENTINE'S WINDOW AT *STEUBEN GLASS*, ZURICH, ARE NOT JUST A USEFUL
PROP BUT ARE AN INTEGRAL PART OF THE SCHEME, FOR THEY ARE SHAPED LIKE
CUPID'S ARROWS. ANOTHER *STEUBEN* WINDOW, BOTTOM, SAYS THE MESSAGE WITH
FLOWERS, ARRANGED ON THE BACK WALL. THE GREEN IVY PROVIDES A STRONG
CONTRAST TO THE RED BACKGROUND.

STEUBEN GLASS, ZURICH, USE THE SAYING 'THE KEY TO MY HEART' LITERALLY
IN THIS DRAMATIC WINDOW DISPLAY FEATURING A LARGE HEART LOCKED IN
CHAINS, KEYS SCATTERED ON THE FLOOR, AND WITH THE ULTIMATE GIFT - A
DIAMOND - AT ITS CENTRE.

A COLOURFUL WINDOW SCHEME FROM *LANE CRAWFORD*, HONG KONG. THE LARGE TARGET POSITIONED ON THE BACK WALL DRAWS THE EYE, AND THE OBLIGATORY HEART IN THE CENTRE SENDS A FUN VALENTINE'S MESSAGE.

RALPH LAUREN, LONDON, PROMOTE THE ANNUAL TENNIS CHAMPIONSHIPS AT WIMBLEDON BY INSTALLING A TRADITIONAL WINDOW THAT DETAILS THE OCCASION. THE GREEN AND WHITE PAVILION ACTS AS A STRONG, RECOGNIZABLE BACKDROP FOR THE MANNEQUINS.

QUIRKY

*A LITTLE NONSENSE NOW AND
THEN IS RELISHED BY THE
WISEST MEN.*
ROALD DAHL

Some window displays don't fall into a conventional commercial retail category, whose aim is simply to sell. On occasion a fashion maestro or pioneering visual merchandiser will break with tradition and produce a show-stopping installation that really challenges the customer. These windows can be perceived as surreal, artistic or quirky.

The *Oxford English Dictionary* describes the word 'quirky' as 'a peculiar behavioural habit; a strange chance occurrence; a sudden twist, turn, or curve'. The peculiar has always held a fascination for people. The early Victorians collected rare objects and displayed them in what was known as a 'cabinet of curiosities'. Over time, some of these collections have developed into the museums we know today. The strange objects that attracted inquisitive individuals were no longer just exhibited in the privacy of their parlours, but were exposed to other eager enthusiasts interested in the quirky and the peculiar. This fascination with displaying the unusual is often reflected in window display, and can give an insight into the imagination of the designer.

To the twenty-first-century shopper, 'quirky' no longer means the unknown, but what they may find interesting and unusual. Rather than shock tactics, a window designer often employs more subtle strategies to win over the customer. One of these is humour, which will undoubtedly fall flat with certain customers. Wit, like art, is subjective; the viewer will not always 'get it'. For most avant-garde designers, a double-take is exactly the reaction they are aiming for.

The Italian fashion designer Franco Moschino launched his label in 1983. His eccentric designs were also the inspiration for his window displays. Long after his death in 1994, his legacy lives on through his window displays. After studying fine art, Moschino had ambitions of being a painter, and judging by his windows he must have spent time studying the Surrealists. One run of Moschino windows showed an army of ants carrying away a bust form wearing a desirable piece of clothing, while the handbag collection was displayed like chocolates nestling in a luxury box, complete with a branded ribbon. There was even a fashion show with stuffed mice as models wearing miniature garments. Inspiring window schemes such as these may or may not promote Moschino's designer collection, but is this really the point? The windows encourage Moschino's customers to buy into his quirky eccentricity.

The British designer Paul Smith has never been shy of exhibiting his sense of humour. His flagship store windows in London's Floral Street are never crammed with products. Smith's confidence is evident in the sparse amount of merchandise he shows, and is reinforced by the clever use of everyday items that make his windows not only quirky, but often thought-provoking. These items range from Michael Jackson to a plastic bag – holding, of course, one of Smith's desirable pieces of luggage – to another of his leather bags with a ladder growing out of it (reminiscent of the most famous British nanny, Mary Poppins, and her magical bag), to a simple plinth with a single bottle of plant food on top of it. Do customers understand each of his abstract window displays? Does he care? His product sells across the globe and he has a cult following because of this quirky style that he portrays with utter confidence. Unlike many who have tried to adopt eccentricity, Smith's seems to come naturally.

A visual merchandiser with a sense of humour who can depict not only fashion trends, but also social trends, with his or her tongue in cheek will always attract controversy. A Selfridges window display in London featuring live pole dancers was shut down by the local council, as was a window designed as part of their 'Las Vegas' promotion. The window featured a large drinking straw attached to an oversized human nose sucking up a dubious white powder. Shock tactics will cause a reaction, but not always the right one.

Being able to stimulate the customer's imagination not just with an artistic representation of the product, but by adding a hint of whimsical wit or irony, is an exceptional skill. The Italian design house Fornarina used the windows at la Rinascente, Milan, to promote their collection by introducing fake human skulls and voodoo imagery with, of course, a vampish model posed in the quirky scheme.

Matthew Williamson, the acclaimed British fashion designer for the rich and famous, could adopt a sophisticated yet conservative philosophy for his window displays, using his stunning stores as a backdrop to a mediocre presentation. Instead he uses his open windows as a canvas to enforce both his brand and his creativity. Williamson's windows are more akin to an art installation than to a reliable display that sells. One window display saw mannequins dressed in his couture clothing being eaten by a life-size *Tyrannosaurus rex*. Not many fashion gurus would want their desirable collection to be seen being gobbled up by a prehistoric creature!

On Pedder, the luxury shoe chain in Hong Kong, could proudly display their designer collections in a conventional manner, but they prefer to enlighten their customers with a brilliant sense of humour. A recent display saw a huge meteorite crashing into their windows and crushing everything in its path, including the bust forms and fixtures. Surprisingly, the only thing that survived was the pair of desirable shoes positioned at the front of the window in view of the passers-by.

A visual merchandiser may not have studied Dalí or Ernst and the Surrealist movement; they may simply have been blessed with a sense of humour, which they bring to the fore in their window displays. For retailers aiming to force their product on the unsuspecting consumer, a visual merchandiser with a strong sense of the absurd can make the journey a little less serious and a lot more fun.

AN INNOVATIVE METHOD OF DISPLAYING A RANGE OF HANDBAGS FOR *TOPSHOP*, LONDON. THIS FOREST OF ELONGATED ARMS IS THE PERFECT TOOL TO SHOW THE SEASON'S MUST-HAVE FASHION ACCESSORY.

A WINDOW DISPLAY FROM *HENRI BENDEL*, NEW YORK, THAT CHALLENGES THE
VIEWER TO LOOK MORE CLOSELY AT THE DECORATIONS ADORNING THE WINDOW:
A TREE MADE OF RED DOLLS FILLS THE SPACE IN ONE SECTION, WHERE A RED GIRL
LOOKS THROUGH TO HER ALTER EGO ON THE OTHER SIDE.

PAUL SMITH HAS ALWAYS DEMONSTRATED A SENSE OF QUIRKINESS IN HIS CONTEMPORARY FASHION DESIGN, AND HIS FLAGSHIP STORE IN LONDON ALSO PROJECTS THIS HUMOUR. HIS CONFIDENCE IS CLEAR – RATHER THAN FORCING HIS PRODUCT ONTO HIS CUSTOMER, HE QUESTIONS IF THEY UNDERSTAND HIS OUTLANDISH ECCENTRICITY.

THE LATE, GREAT ITALIAN DESIGNER *FRANCO MOSCHINO*, NOTED FOR HIS QUIRKY
CREATIONS, ALSO PROVED TO HIS AUDIENCE THROUGH HIS WINDOWS THAT
FASHION SHOULD BE FUN. THIS DISPLAY, APTLY CALLED 'CARRIED AWAY',
IN HIS MILAN STORE, ILLUSTRATES AN ARMY OF ANTS RUNNING AWAY
WITH A CATWALK CREATION.

A *MOSCHINO*, MILAN, WINDOW THAT PRESENTS A NON-EDIBLE COLLECTION OF CHOCOLATES. THE HANDBAGS PRESENTED IN A GIFT BOX LOOK GOOD ENOUGH TO EAT!

ANTHROPOLOGIE, NEW YORK, HAVE ADOPTED A HONEY-BEAR THEME IN THIS SET OF WINDOWS. THE SCHEME PLAYS NOT ONLY ON THE PRODUCTION OF THE BEES' NECTAR BUT ALSO, AMUSINGLY, THE FINISHED BOTTLED PRODUCT. THE CLEVER USE OF HONEY SUSPENDED IN BEAR-SHAPED SQUEEZY BOTTLES IS JUST ONE OF THE INNOVATIVE IDEAS THAT HAS BEEN CARRIED THROUGH THE OTHER WINDOWS.

A FUN WINDOW FROM *MOSCHINO*, MILAN, BELOW, WITH MICE MODELLING ON AN OVERSIZED RUNWAY WATCHED BY MOUSE FASHION WRITERS. BOTTOM, ANOTHER OFFERING FROM *MOSCHINO*, MILAN, THIS TIME A SURREAL WINDOW CONTAINING A BUST FORM ON TOP OF AN APARTMENT BUILDING. THE VIEWER IS LEFT TO PONDER OVER THE CONCEPT.

A STUNNING WINDOW DISPLAY FROM BRITISH DESIGNER *MATTHEW WILLIAMSON*
– HIS LONDON STORE PROMOTES HIS COUTURE COLLECTION WITH AN ABUNDANCE
OF ALARM CLOCKS COVERING THE FLOOR.

SKULLS AND ROSES ARE THE MAIN THEME IN THIS *FORNARINA* WINDOW DISPLAY AT *LA RINASCENTE*, MILAN. THE STRONG FASHION STATEMENT WORKS IN CONTRAST WITH THE SINISTER VISUAL CONCEPT.

AN IMPRESSIVE AND ORIGINAL WINDOW INSTALLATION AT *HARVEY NICHOLS*, LONDON. A MASSIVE DINOSAUR CRAWLS THROUGH THE WINDOWS, MADE ENTIRELY OF COAT HANGERS STRATEGICALLY POSITIONED TO GIVE THE IMPRESSION OF MOVEMENT. THE HANGERS ATTACHED TO THE MANNEQUINS' HEADS ARE AN INNOVATIVE ALTERNATIVE TO WIGS.

A GIANT STACK OF PLAYING CARDS TUMBLES TO THE FLOOR IN THIS *ON PEDDER* WINDOW, HONG KONG, TO CREATE A DYNAMIC WINDOW DISPLAY FOR THEIR DESIGNER SHOES. THE LARGE CARDS EVEN FORM A PLATFORM TO SUPPORT THE CHIC FOOTWEAR.

THIS SUPERHERO'S TORSO IN THE WINDOW OF *ON PEDDER*, HONG KONG, ACTS
AS AN IMPRESSIVE PROP TO PROMOTE THE LUXURY SHOES. A BOLD AND BIZARRE
STATEMENT SUCH AS THIS IS AN EFFECTIVE WAY TO GAIN AN INQUISITIVE
REACTION FROM THE PUBLIC.

A GIANT METEORITE HAS LANDED IN THE WINDOWS OF *ON PEDDER*,
HONG KONG, UNFORTUNATELY CRUSHING A MANNEQUIN AND CAUSING
THE WINDOW SCHEME TO COLLAPSE, YET THE DESIGNER SHOES STAY INTACT
IN FULL VIEW OF THE CUSTOMERS.

A FUN WINDOW FROM *HENRI BENDEL*, NEW YORK, CREATED TO PROMOTE THE DESIGNER *NORMA KAMALI*, WHERE LIGHTWEIGHT MANNEQUINS APPEAR TO FLOAT FROM THEIR BUBBLEGUM BUBBLES.

THIS SURREAL WINDOW SCHEME FROM *HARRODS*, LONDON, HAS A BACKDROP OF
EYES THAT HIGHLIGHTS THE MANNEQUIN GROUPING. THE DECAL ON THE GLASS
IS A CLEVER WAY TO FRAME THE WINDOW AND ENFORCE THE THEME.

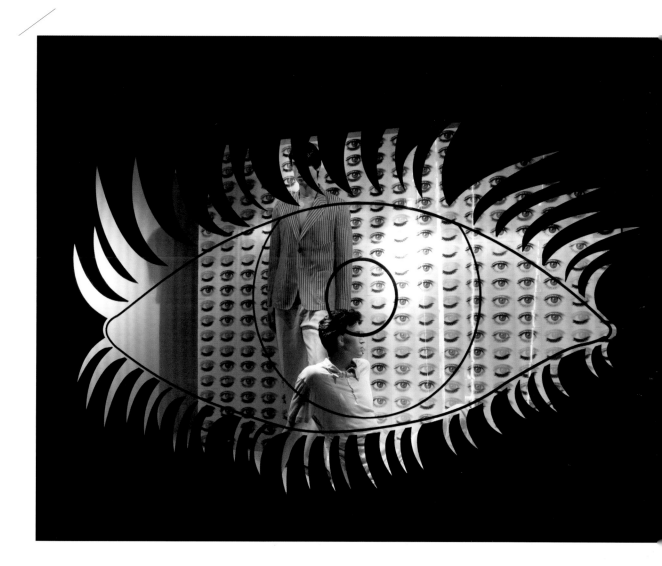

A STYLISH MODEL IS EATEN IN THIS *MATTHEW WILLIAMSON* SCHEME, LONDON.
THESE QUIRKY WINDOWS MOCK HIGH FASHION AND SHOW WILLIAMSON'S
CONFIDENCE IN HIS COLLECTION. NOT EVERY DESIGNER WOULD APPRECIATE
THEIR MERCHANDISE BEING SHOWN IN SUCH A BRUTAL AND LAUGHABLE MANNER.

THESE INSPIRING WINDOWS FROM *HARVEY NICHOLS*, LONDON, WERE PART OF A SCHEME CALLED 'URBAN JUNGLE'. EACH WINDOW SAW LARGER-THAN-LIFE EXOTIC ANIMALS INTERACTING WITH MANNEQUINS DRESSED IN DESIGNER CLOTHING THAT CONTRASTED WITH THE UNUSUAL SETTING.

A CLEVER WINDOW DISPLAY FROM *PRINTEMPS*, PARIS, THAT SHOWS A MANNEQUIN
LADEN DOWN WITH SHOPPING BAGS PRINTED WITH THE STORE'S LOGO. THE
GOLD SHOPPING TROLLEY AND MANNEQUIN CREATE AN ORIGINAL CONCEPT
FOR A LUXURY DEPARTMENT STORE, THE TROLLEY BEING MORE AT HOME IN
A SUPERMARKET.

A MANNEQUIN IS SUSPENDED IN CHAINS IN THIS THOUGHT-PROVOKING *HARVEY NICHOLS*, LONDON, WINDOW DISPLAY. THE OVERSIZED PADLOCKS AND BIZARRE SHADOW MAKE A MOCKERY OF THE UNFORTUNATE MANNEQUIN.

HOLT RENFREW, TORONTO, TOOK A CIRCUS THEME FOR THIS RUN OF SHOW-STOPPING WINDOWS WITH ACROBAT MANNEQUINS PERFORMING AGAINST A TENTED BACKDROP. THE MIX OF REAL GYMNASTIC EQUIPMENT AND OTHER PROPS WITH THE ELABORATELY MASKED MODELS LENDS A SURREAL AIR.

AGENT PROVOCATEUR DISPLAY THEIR TYPICALLY BRITISH SENSE OF HUMOUR. THIS WINDOW IN THEIR LONDON STORE HAS A CHEEKY MANNEQUIN COMICALLY SQUEEZING ICING FROM AN OVERSIZED PIPING BAG.

A QUIRKY PLAY ON WORDS IN THE *AGENT PROVOCATEUR* WINDOW, LONDON. *KATE MOSS* IS USED IN A SERIES OF PICTURES TO PROMOTE THEIR LINGERIE, WHILE A CAKE REMINDS THE VIEWER OF THE ORIGINS OF THE SLOGAN.

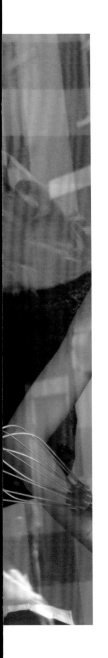

TRENDS

*FASHION IS BORN BY SMALL FACTS,
TRENDS, OR EVEN POLITICS,
NEVER BY TRYING TO MAKE LITTLE
PLEATS AND FURBELOWS, BY
TRINKETS, BY CLOTHES EASY
TO COPY, OR BY THE SHORTENING
OR LENGTHENING OF A SKIRT.*
ELSA SCHIAPARELLI

Translating fashion trends into window displays is a key skill for a visual merchandiser. Whether a store specializes in high-street clothing or designer wear, food or homewares, a visual merchandiser will have an understanding of their customers' style aspirations and spending habits. They are accustomed to reacting quickly to consumer trends and designing windows that will inspire their customers to own the latest style items, whether to wear or to dress their home with.

Having an awareness of future trends is also essential. A window stylist will follow the catwalk shows with great enthusiasm, not only to replicate the trends but to adapt them for customers who may not be able to afford these costly collections. Their commercial yet creative eye will focus on the length of hemlines but also on the accessories each model wears on the runway. An important fashion show from a noted designer will give a visual merchandiser a head start with their planning, as the product featured on the runway will not appear in-store until six months later. By that time they will have researched the trends for the following season. Visual merchandisers can keep track of the evolving catwalk trends from Paris, Milan, London and New York by logging on to fashion websites, many of which upload fashion-show images as soon as the last model leaves the runway. They will also take note of the music and choreography, as well as the stage that was designed to show the collections. Each of these valuable elements may be vital for a future window presentation. Visual merchandisers often attend trend forecasting shows, such as Première Vision in Paris, hoping to tune into future fashion trends along with the designers.

Details such as the mannequins' wigs and make-up are never overlooked when creating a window that is a high-fashion statement. They are planned long in advance, along with the overall window scheme. Mannequins can be renovated to suit the clothing that they are destined to carry. These Amazonian fibreglass figures are resprayed and remodelled with appropriate wigs for each appearance, and even nail colour will be discussed. Male and child models also succumb to this seasonal makeover.

The importance of attaining the correct look for the mannequins, just as for the models on the catwalk, is paramount. On occasions a retailer will not only emulate the trends of a catwalk presentation, but may duplicate the complete scene. Selfridges, London, not only took inspiration from Alexander McQueen's 2008 Autumn/Winter collection, but recreated the catwalk show in their largest window, with a delicately lit swathe of fabric acting as a centrepiece and stylized mannequins that could have graced his runway. A collaboration such as this, between designer and retailer, allows the brand's image to be represented as the designer intended.

A window stylist will often recreate a fashion look, either using the original designer product or a less expensive version, and the British high street is testimony to this practice. There are no legal implications for simply following a trend, but using a designer's name or brand logo without consent could cause legal issues. On most occasions a brand will be more than happy to help a store promote their products, also ensuring that their brand image is enforced. Printemps in Paris collaborated with the world's most famous fashion magazine, *Vogue*, for their 'Rock Culture' windows, with the word 'Vogue' being the main prop. Covered in sequins and glitter, it acted as a simple but striking backdrop.

A confident fashion statement will always attract customers. Dressing a mannequin in the must-have seasonal fashion statement is a confident way of drawing shoppers into a store. The Belgian designer Dries Van Noten does not require lavish props to help sell his clothing; his designer collections are shown simply on a bust form that his customers can admire, and hopefully aspire to own.

Many high-end designer stores rely solely on advertising to promote themselves, whereas high-street stores will use seasonal trends and a reputation for being quick to embrace those trends to enhance their own fashion credibility. Zara, for example, display their products with the inspiration of Gucci or Prada in mind, but with a different price tag. This Spanish retail leader has mastered the art of window styling – their signature monochromatic window schemes are always successful with European fashionistas. Mango, Bershka and H&M, among others, have all recruited visual merchandisers who have not only a good eye for fashion but an understanding of styling mannequins in the latest trends.

Luxury fashion houses have in the past relied solely on the cachet of their couture collections to entice the wealthy into their ready-to-wear boutiques. Today, even these trendsetters are drawing on their creativity to produce stylish window displays. Prada in Milan created a mirrored structure complete with pillars and columns for one of their Christmas windows, with the signature mannequin in the centre immaculately dressed in Prada's finest clothing. This concept framed the merchandise in an elegant and sophisticated manner. Their 'Techno Cave' scheme saw mannequins positioned in the centre of a window shrouded by hundreds of pieces of broken mirror.

A window dedicated to just one designer portrays a strong fashion statement because the merchandise or theme is not diluted with other brands. Such windows can easily be focused on the fashion designer's aspirations for their brand and the trends that they set, thus satisfying the designer and informing the customer. Mixing brands together to create universal trends can be achieved by experienced window stylists in department stores, which sell a range of brands, but a simple presentation from one designer will be enough to help sell a collection. Dolce&Gabbana used la Rinascente's windows in Milan to showcase the season's must-have handbag. One designer, one handbag: the impact would have been diluted if the window also featured bags from other designers.

There is no doubt that following fashion trends is important for a visual merchandiser specializing in fashion, but trends are vital in other areas of retail too. A home, food or cosmetic visual merchandiser will also need to be aware of movements within their industry. It is no longer just about the shape, style and size of the product, but about who is wearing, eating or talking about it. A successful visual merchandiser gathers the trends from their customers and competitors as well as the obvious catwalk shows. The internet has made this task easier, with sites predicting trends and updating the surfer with the most recent store openings.

THE SIMPLE BEAUTY OF A POPPY FLOWER TO REPLACE THE HEAD
OF THIS MANNEQUIN FOR *KENZO* IS DRAMATIC AND EYE-CATCHING
AT *PRINTEMPS*, PARIS.

raldine GONZALEZ

étage 0 & éta

A *VIVIENNE WESTWOOD* DESIGNER DRESS HANGS IN A PROTECTIVE BUBBLE
IN THIS *SELFRIDGES* WINDOW, LONDON. COORDINATING ACCESSORIES HANG
NEARBY IN SMALLER GLOBES.

'ROCK CULTURE', A SET OF WINDOWS FROM *PRINTEMPS*, PARIS, THAT PROMOTES A STRONG FASHION CONCEPT SIMPLY BY COLLABORATING WITH THE MOST FAMOUS FASHION MAGAZINE IN THE WORLD: *VOGUE*.

DOLCE&GABBANA PROMOTE THE SEASON'S MOST WANTED HANDBAG AT
LA RINASCENTE, MILAN. PILING THIS COSTLY ITEM HIGH SENDS A QUIRKY MESSAGE
TO THE FASHIONISTAS.

A STUNNING REPRODUCTION OF AN AUTUMN/WINTER *ALEXANDER McQUEEN*
FASHION SHOW INSPIRED BY THE BRITISH EMPIRE IN A *SELFRIDGES*, LONDON,
WINDOW DISPLAY. THE MANNEQUINS APPEAR TO BE MODELLING IN THE ACTUAL
FASHION SHOW.

TWO INNOVATIVE WINDOWS FROM *SAKS FIFTH AVENUE*, NEW YORK. THE SCHEME
IN EACH OF THE WINDOWS HAS BEEN MADE FROM CAREFULLY FOLDED PIECES
OF PAPER FASHIONED INTO BOATS, SOME MATCHING ONE MANNEQUIN'S DRESS.

SELFRIDGES, LONDON, GOES PUNK WITH A DRAMATIC WINDOW DISPLAY TO REINFORCE THEIR 'ATELIER' PROMOTION. COMBINING MOHICANS AND CONTEMPORARY FASHION MAKES A STRONG DESIGN STATEMENT THAT REPRESENTS THE DIVERSITY OF LONDON'S STREET FASHION HERITAGE.

A SIMPLE AND BEAUTIFUL BACKDROP OF FLOWERS USED EN MASSE IN THIS *MARC JACOBS,* NEW YORK, WINDOW CONFIDENTLY PROMOTES A SPRING/SUMMER COLLECTION.

THE DESIGNER *MARIA LUISA* SHOWCASES HER FASHION COLLECTION AT *PRINTEMPS*, PARIS. MANNEQUINS, COMPLETE WITH RUBBER HEADGEAR, STRIKE DRAMATIC POSES TO EMPHASIZE THE LINES OF THE DRESSES, WHILE ANOTHER TAKES A COLLECTION OF DESIGNER SHOES FOR A WALK!

THESE ELEGANT CHRISTMAS WINDOWS IN THE *PRADA* STORE, MILAN, HAVE BEEN DESIGNED TO FRAME THE SINGLE MANNEQUIN. ACCESSORIES HAVE BEEN GROUPED EITHER SIDE TO COORDINATE WITH THE OUTFIT.

ON PEDDER, HONG KONG, USED OVERSIZED TRADITIONAL CHINESE CERAMIC
VASES AS PROPS IN THIS WINDOW TO PROMOTE THE FRENCH SHOE DESIGNER
CHRISTIAN LOUBOUTIN.

PRADA'S 'TECHNO CAVE' WINDOW SCHEME IN MILAN IS MADE UP OF HUNDREDS OF PIECES OF MIRROR. THE DRAMATIC USE OF MIRRORS EN MASSE GROUPED AROUND A SINGLE MANNEQUIN FRAMES THE WINDOW AND FOCUSES THE EYE ON THE FASHION.

THE POSITIONING OF THESE MANNEQUINS WEARING *VALENTINO* IN *LA RINASCENTE*, MILAN, CREATES IMPACT BECAUSE THEY MAKE USE OF THE FULL HEIGHT OF THE STORE'S WINDOW.

A SOPHISTICATED WINDOW FROM *SAKS FIFTH AVENUE*, NEW YORK. TWO DRAMATICALLY POSED MANNEQUINS AND THE BRAND NAME '*DIOR*' ARE ALL THAT IS NEEDED TO PROMOTE THE FRENCH DESIGNER'S COLLECTION.

THESE SIMPLE BUST FORMS USED TO DISPLAY A ***DRIES VAN NOTEN*** DRESS ARE ALL THAT IS NEEDED TO PROMOTE THE DESIGNER'S COLLECTION IN THE *MINISTRY OF CULTURE*, ONE OF THE MOST PRESTIGIOUS PARISIAN WINDOWS. ON THIS OCCASION, KEEPING IT SIMPLE WORKS!

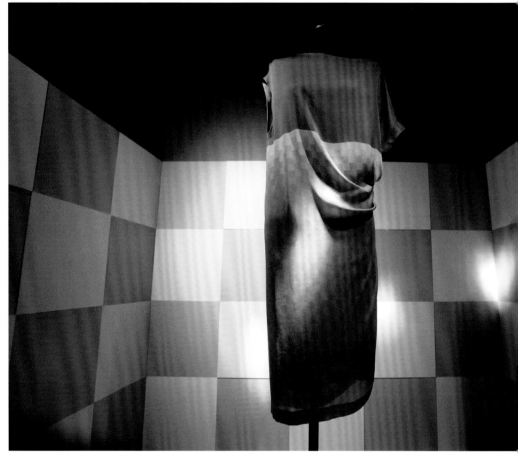

A COLLECTION OF *DRIES VAN NOTEN* WINDOWS IN THE *MINISTRY OF CULTURE*, PARIS, HAS A SIMPLE BUT EFFECTIVE BACKGROUND MADE UP OF SQUARES THAT REFLECT THE CHECK PATTERNS ON THE CLOTHING.

TWO WINDOWS CREATED IN *SAKS FIFTH AVENUE*, NEW YORK, TO PROMOTE THE
FRENCH DESIGNER BRAND *YVES SAINT LAURENT*. THE ELEGANT MODELS ARE
POSING NEXT TO THE HARD LINES OF WHITE CONTEMPORARY STRUCTURES.

A DRAMATIC MANNEQUIN POSES IN FRONT OF AN ELABORATE STRUCTURE OF WOVEN WOOD AT *SAKS FIFTH AVENUE*, NEW YORK. THE SIMPLICITY OF THE PROPS HIGHLIGHTS THE FASHION ELEMENT.

PICTURE CREDITS

**THE PUBLISHER WOULD LIKE TO THANK
THE FOLLOWING PICTURE SOURCES:**

p5 /Robert Stadler, photo Marc Domage
p6 /Andrew Meredith
p11–12 /Michael Taylor
p13 /© Inditex
p14–15 /Francis Peyrat
p16 /Andrew Meredith
p17 /Courtesy of Jaeger, photo Andrew Peppard
p18 /Andrew Meredith
p19 /Melvyn Vincent www.melvynvincent.com
p20–21 /Francis Peyrat
p22–23 /Andrew Meredith
p24 /© Inditex
p25 /Topshop
p26–27 /Andrew Meredith
p28–29 /Francis Peyrat
p30–31 /Topshop
p32–33 / © D.R.
p34 /Topshop
p35 /Michael Taylor
p36–37 /Andrew Meredith
p38 /Topshop
p41 /Topshop
p42–43 /Francis Peyrat
p44 /Nienke Kinder
p45 /Topshop
p46–52 /Andrew Meredith
p53–54 /Topshop
p55 /Michael Taylor
p56 /Topshop
p57–58–59 /Melvyn Vincent www.melvynvincent.com
p60 /Francis Peyrat
p61 /Louis Vuitton, photo Jamie Cabreza
/www.jamiecabreza.com
p62–63 /Topshop

p64 /www.fornarina.com
p65 /Melvyn Vincent www.melvynvincent.com
p66 /James Doiron
p67 /Topshop
p68 /Melvyn Vincent www.melvynvincent.com
p69 /Courtesy of Henri Bendel
p70 /Topshop
p71 /Courtesy of Henri Bendel
p72–75–76 /Andrew Meredith
p77 /Francis Peyrat
p78–79–80–81–82–83 /Andrew Meredith
p84 /Francis Peyrat
p85 /Angelo Merendino
p86–87 /Owen Thomas
p88–89 /Louis Vuitton, photo Jamie Cabreza
/www.jamiecabreza.com
p90 /Melvyn Vincent www.melvynvincent.com
p91 /Andrew Meredith
p92–93 /Courtesy of Robert Stadler, photo
Marc Domage
p94 /Lawrence Patti
p97 /Andrew Meredith
p98–99 /Bergdorf Goodman
p100 / © D.R.
p101 /Topshop
p102–103 /Andrew Meredith
p104 /Bergdorf Goodman
p105–106–107 /Andrew Meredith
p108 /James Doiron
p109 /Michael Taylor
p110 /Courtesy of Polo Ralph Lauren
p111 /Melvyn Vincent www.melvynvincent.com
p112–113 /Francis Peyrat
p114 /Lawrence Patti
p115 /Andrew Meredith
p116–117 /Bergdorf Goodman
p118–121–122–123 /Andrew Meredith
p124 /Courtesy of Polo Ralph Lauren

p125 /Courtesy of Barneys New York
p126–127 /Andrew Meredith
p128 /Melvyn Vincent www.melvynvincent.com
p129 /© D.R.
p130 /Francis Peyrat
p131 /James Doiron
p132 /Courtesy of Moschino
p133 /Angelo Merendino
p134–135 /© Matthew Williamson
p136–137 /Angelo Merendino
p138 /Lane Crawford Hong Kong
p139 /Courtesy of Polo Ralph Lauren
p140 /© Matthew Williamson
p143 /Topshop
p144 /Courtesy of Henri Bendel
p145 /Courtesy of Paul Smith Ltd.
p146–147 /Courtesy of Moschino
p148 /Rebecca Borenstein, Elizabeth Felicella
p149 /Courtesy of Moschino
p150 /© Matthew Williamson
p151 /www.fornarina.com
p152–153 /Michael Taylor
p154–155–156–157 /Joseph Cheung
p158 /Courtesy of Henri Bendel
p159 /Melvyn Vincent www.melvynvincent.com
p160 /© Matthew Williamson
p161 /Michael Taylor
p162 /Francis Peyrat
p163 /Michael Taylor
p 164–165 /James Doiron
p166–167 /Enzo Peccinotti
p168 /Courtesy of Dries Van Noten
p171 /Francis Peyrat
p172 /Andrew Meredith
p173 /Francis Peyrat
p174 /Courtesy of la Rinascente
p175 /Andrew Meredith
p176 /Courtesy of Saks Fifth Avenue New York

p177 /Andrew Meredith
p178 /Leon Neal/Getty Images
p179 /Francis Peyrat
p180 /Courtesy of Prada
p181 /Joseph Cheung
p182–183 /Courtesy of Prada
p184 /James Doiron
p185 /Courtesy of la Rinascente
p186–187 /Courtesy of Dries Van Noten
p188–189 /Courtesy of Saks Fifth Avenue New York